NEW MEXICO
GHOST
TOWNS

NEW MEXICO GHOST TOWNS

Donna Blake Birchell

THE
History
PRESS

Published by The History Press
Charleston, SC
www.historypress.com

All images are courtesy of the author unless otherwise indicated.

First published 2022

Manufactured in the United States

ISBN 9781467148269

Library of Congress Control Number: 2021950575

For all those who pioneered a wild, strange land to establish an enhanced way of life for others and bettered themselves along the same route.

——————

There is a deep sense in which we are all ghost towns. We are all haunted by the memory of those we love, those with whom we feel we have unfinished business. While they may no longer be with us, a faint aroma of their presence remains, a presence that haunts us until we make our peace with them and let them go.

—*Peter Rollins*

CONTENTS

CONTENTS

ACKNOWLEDGEMENTS

As always, many thanks go to Samantha Villa, who believed in me more than I did myself. I will truly always be grateful, my sweet friend.

It goes without saying that without the great outpouring of love and encouragement from my wonderful family, Jerry, Michael, and Justin, I would not be able to continue this long journey. You are all the best, and I could not have done this without your support. Sending you much love and a huge thank-you from the bottom of my heart.

Many thanks to my dear friends Richard and Carol Estes for your encouragement and excitement. I think you are more excited about the books than I am!

Amy McVay Tellez and John LeMay of the Historical Museum of Roswell, you both hold a special place in my heart for the many blessings of friendship you have brought into my life! I am not worthy!

To my editor, Ben Gibson, thank you for the gentle guidance and freedom to create. To all the unsung heroes at Arcadia Publishing who work diligently to produce the best books possible—I am truly indebted to you.

I owe a huge debt of gratitude to all of you, who take time out of your lives to read my humble words. Your support and encouragement mean so much—thank you isn't enough!

INTRODUCTION

New Mexico is a wild, open land full of varied landscapes and diverse cultures. The Native cultures were the first to cultivate this terrain, adding their own special touches to the stunning backdrop. When the Spaniards arrived in 1598 to settle, they also changed the complexion of New Mexico with their architectural style and religious beliefs. But it was most likely the Anglo population, who came west to homestead and find their fortunes in gold, who changed the entire aspect of the New Mexico Territory for the Indigenous people. The Native tribes were pushed aside, their lands confiscated and their way of life eradicated, all in the name of progress. Although these events happened over two to four hundred years ago, the scars are still painful for Native communities.

Brave souls from the eastern part of the United States ventured into the unknown to cash in—quite literally, in many cases—on the seemingly limitless opportunities before them in the western territories. The lure of the precious metals available made many rich beyond their wildest imagination and others broken irreparably. The West was hard on those who were not prepared for the lessons it would teach. It was also a haven for outlaws, con men, shady ladies—each with a plan to separate the prospectors from their gold. The West was treacherous to say the least.

What constitutes a ghost town? According to sources, a true ghost town is a completely abandoned settlement. This book will feature many little-known towns that are no more than a foundation, as well as those still inhabited by a limited population. Although the word *ghost* implies that a place is haunted, only a select few have gained this reputation—many for good reason. We ask when you visit a town with a population that you be as unintrusive as possible, for this is their home.

FROZEN IN TIME

Remnants of over four hundred of these settlements can be found in nearly every part of New Mexico, especially along the Rio Grande Corridor, where mining was most prevalent. Often, only ruins remain of what were once bustling communities, full of life. If the adobe and wooden walls left in these towns could speak, we would most likely hear a raucous tale to make us blush. The fact these structures, many built from the delicate material of adobe, have stood the test of time for future generations to explore and ponder is amazing. Many times, the rate these towns grew was astonishing, so the construction was hasty and possibly less than sturdy—not up to today's standards for sure.

We are grateful for the glimpses into the past that are frozen in time, showing us insight into the hard work and determination it took to forge a life in the woolly West. New Mexico is a stunningly gorgeous state with much to offer its visitors, but it can be less than forgiving to those who try to uncover its treasures. Weather changes often occur several times daily in the state. Droughts, torrential rains, wind and heavy snows plagued the settlers. They were truly the epitome of the old saying "what doesn't kill you makes you stronger."

How do once-thriving communities become ghost towns? As you travel to the small settlements you read about here, you will notice it looks like some of the townspeople just vanished or picked up and moved in an extreme hurry. Pans were left on the stove, dishes were left with food on the tables, children's toys were discarded in haste. One of the reasons for this in New Mexico was a diphtheria epidemic, outbreaks of which were reported in rural parts of the state from 1910 to 1915. Influenza also ravaged the state in 1918—both were mostly uncontrolled and caused many deaths, especially in children, which also resulted in small towns being nearly wiped out. The lonely cemeteries you still can visit are filled with these victims.

The railroad was the other factor that made towns either boom or bust. As towns were bypassed by the steel rails, there was no other way for the residents to get their goods to market without traveling by wagon for days at a time. Often, the items were spoiled and unusable by the time they reached the railyards. Being passed by the railroad was the kiss of death for these once-prosperous towns.

GOLD RUSHES

Everyone is aware of the gold rush in California in 1849, which saw throngs of prospectors, family men and tender feet rush to the Golden State to make their fortunes, but few know that New Mexico also had a gold rush of its own. In fact, the first gold rush west of the Mississippi River occurred in the New Mexico Territory in 1820, when the shiny yellow metal was discovered in the San Pedro Mountains, east of Golden. Gold mines in the state were both placer and lode mines, producing millions of dollars in revenue during their tenure. According to author Virginia T. McLemore, between the years of 1848 to 2000, more than 3.2 million ounces of gold and 117 million ounces of silver have been produced in New Mexico.

Towns like Golden, Los Cerrillos and Madrid popped up along what is now known as the Turquoise Trail, because gold was not the only treasure found in the surrounding mountains. Turquoise, copper, lead, tin, zinc and silver were also heavily mined. Turquoise, the state gem, is highly prized by the Native people as a stone with great healing properties.

By 1879, the southwestern part of the state saw an influx of miners prospecting for silver and gold. The towns of Hillsboro, Lake Valley and Kingston blossomed as the amount of ore pulled from the surrounding hills increased as well. The infamous madam Sadie Orchard set up shop and several enterprises in these towns and the Black Range Mountains, as she was never one to miss an opportunity.

Many of these sites are mining-related, since the discovery of precious metals, minerals and turquoise seemed to be a daily event in the late 1800s. All but six New Mexico counties are represented by at least one ghost town in this book, the others, unfortunately, have towns which are only memories.

SILVER PANIC OF 1893

The United States was in an economic depression in 1893, and it lasted until 1897, causing a political realignment in 1896 with the election of President William McKinley. Between 1870 and 1900—the Gilded Age—the country

The Bridal Chamber Mine in Lake Valley pulled 2.5 million ounces of silver from the ground.

Silver ore—not impressive to look at but valuable.

saw rapid economic growth, particularly in the northern and western states. This prosperity relied heavily on high international commodity prices, and there were some hiccups along the way.

In 1893, wheat prices crashed, but the silver mines in the West were producing ore in enormous quantities, which led to a debate about how much of this silver could be used for coinage and if the mines could continue extracting the product at a profit. With the enactment of the Sherman Silver Purchase Act of 1890, the miners were hoping to encourage the government to increase the demand for silver; under this act, the United States government purchased millions of ounces of silver with issues of paper currency. In accordance with the 1878 Bland-Allison Act, the government was required to purchase these millions of ounces, which drove up the price of silver. This made America the second-largest buyer of silver in the world (the British Crown was the first, as the Indian rupee was backed by silver instead of gold). People were attempting to redeem silver notes for gold, so the statutory limit for gold reserves was reached and notes could no longer be redeemed for gold.

Demand for silver and silver notes fell, thus devaluing silver significantly. This caused runs on the banks, as people rushed to withdraw their funds before a collapse. Many bank and railroad failures followed. The bankruptcy of over fifteen thousand companies and five hundred banks—mainly in the western states—caused high unemployment and a panic, which caused a trickledown effect on other aspects of life, including shipping and supply.

So, when the silver-rich mines of New Mexico were pulling ore, it was then worth mere pennies—not worth the efforts of mining anymore. The closure of the mines caused the deaths of many towns that supported the mining operations, leaving us with ghost towns to explore.

VISITING GHOST TOWNS

The allure of riches is still strong today, and while we encourage you to explore these fascinating sites, we would also ask that you please use caution when walking around the abandoned buildings and mineshafts. A vast majority of the ghost towns mentioned in this book are on public land and require no permits or passes to enjoy, but for those few which are on private land, please respect the wishes of the landowner and either gain permission to enter or view from a distance. Trespassing is a crime and can come with a hefty fine. Remember, although these buildings are vacant and derelict, they do have owners, so please take only photographs and memories from your visits.

While most of the residents may be there in spirit only, be mindful of the wildlife that calls these old structures home. A bite from a rattlesnake, centipede, scorpion or recluse spider can quickly ruin a great outing. Mountain lions, bobcats, coyotes, badgers and bears can also be found roaming in most of the state and may be looking for a cool place to rest out of the New Mexico sun.

Old water wells and abandoned mine shafts, which can be partially hidden by vegetation, pose one of the greatest hazards while out exploring, as they can be hundreds of feet deep and in some cases do not have a grate over their opening. Tailing piles are usually not supported, so they can give way at any time, causing a landslide. Please be sure to have plenty of extra water, first aid supplies and food with you—as well as a full tank of fuel—for your journeys throughout the state, as most of the locations are in isolated regions.

LAND OF ENCHANTMENT

New Mexico's vast landscape and creative vibe has long won the hearts of those who are lucky enough to live within its borders and those who are drawn to visit. After joining the Union on January 6, 1912, New Mexico has long had an identity crisis, as it gets overlooked on many occasions. For those who live here, we know the wonders that await visitors to our greatly varied sceneries, and it is this writer's hope that through this book, others will be enticed to visit and discover the Land of Enchantment for themselves.

PART I

NORTH-CENTRAL AND CENTRAL NEW MEXICO

1

SANTA FE COUNTY

BONANZA CITY

35.5389232, -106.1200224

As with many of the New Mexico ghost town sites that will be mentioned in this book, Bonanza City has been used as a movie set by Hollywood. The Bonanza Creek Movie Ranch was built close to the ruins of Bonanza City and has been seen in *Lonesome Dove*, *Silverado*, *Hostiles*, *Wild Hogs*, *Cowboys & Aliens*, *3:10 to Yuma* and *Appaloosa*—to name just a few of the at least 130 movies that have been filmed here. The wide-open spaces surrounding the ranch are also utilized for commercials by companies like the Ford Motor Company™ and Dr. Pepper™.

The initial mining of lead in the Cerrillos Hills was done by the Spaniards in the late 1600s to produce the bullets they thought would be needed for the Reconquista of 1692, but this was sporadic through the 1700s and early 1800s. Cerrillos Hills was owned by Mexico until 1848, when President Ulysses S. Grant began selling the land in New Mexico to the American public.

Bonanza City was a mining town established in 1880 with the discovery of silver and gold in the Cerrillos Hills thirteen miles southwest of the New Mexico capital city of Santa Fe. John Mahoney, who was a former United States counsel to Algiers, is given credit for founding the boom town. The population blossomed to two thousand people by the next year, and the small town included a saloon, church and smelter to service the over five hundred mine shafts in the region.

Cerrillos

35.43664, -106.12963

Also called Los Cerrillos, which means "little hills," the quaint village of Cerrillos looks like a setting for an Old West movie. It was indeed used for that purpose in: *Young Guns*, *Young Guns II*, *The Cowboys*, *Nine Lives of Elfego Baca* and *Outrageous Fortune*. Evidence of these productions—and eight others— are still visible on the building façades along the main dirt road. Aside from the fact you would have arrived in an automobile, you could swear that you crossed a time warp into the 1800s.

According to the New Mexico Bureau of Immigration Report, in 1906, Cerrillos was touted as being the principal settlement of southern Santa Fe County with a smelter, stone quarries, public school building, church, business houses and several mining properties in the vicinity of the town.

Modern history dates the establishment of Cerrillos to 1879, but the area's history dates back more than 1,500 years, when it was the home of Puebloan people, descendants of the Anasazi who lived and mined turquoise

Downtown Cerrillos became Lincoln, New Mexico, in *Young Guns*.

Mary's Bar is a staple in Cerrillos for locals and tourists alike.

there. Although the town does not consider itself to be a ghost town, wishing instead to be seen as an old mining town, Cerrillos fits the definition from *Merriam-Webster*: a "once-flourishing town wholly or nearly deserted, usually as a result of the exhaustion of some natural resource." In Cerrillos's case, its abandonment was the result of the exhaustion of multiple resources, namely gold, silver, copper, zinc, lead and turquoise.

Turquoise has been mined in the Cerrillos area in twelve different locations along the slopes of Turquoise Hill and Mount Chalchihuitl since 500 CE by the local Native tribes. This sky-blue gemstone has risen in value and use since then, quickly becoming embedded with New Mexico's personality as the official state gemstone. New Mexico is known as the land of a thousand volcanos, and this volcanic activity produced large deposits of the gemstone throughout the state. The relatively soft stone is commonly found in arid desert regions in the company of copper within one hundred feet of the surface. Egypt—the southwest edge of the Sinai Peninsula to be more precise—is the site of the oldest turquoise (which was called mufkat by the Egyptians) mine in the world, dating back three thousand years.

Mount Chalchihuitl was said to have been the largest mining operation of the prehistoric era, as well as the largest single deposit of the precious stone in North America. *Chalchihuitl* (pronounced chal-che-we'-tl) is a derivative of the Nahua/Aztec word that means "blue-green." The mountain, although it has one of the smallest deposits, is the most important and has been registered in the New Mexico State Register of Cultural Places since January 20, 1978.

History states two Colorado miners found deposits of gold in the Ortiz Mountains in 1879, which immediately acted as a magnet for opportunists and the Santa Fe Railroad. A tent city quickly began to form and could boast a population of eight hundred by 1890, even though the only resource available at that time was coal. Follow NM-14, or the Turquoise Trail, to visit Cerrillos, Golden and Madrid.

DOLORES

35.3425397, -106.1197448

Ancient Puebloans settled in this area until around 1300 CE, as did the Spaniards who passed through the region when the Declaration of Independence was signed in 1776. Gold-rich quartz veins were found around Real de Delores—now Delores—in 1833. During its gold rush, the town grew to a population of approximately 4,000 but dwindled in 1849, when the combination of the California gold rush and rumors of more gold in the San Pedro Mountains began drawing miners away. By 1870, there were only 150 people left in the town.

Gold in the New Mexico Territory was so attractive that big leaguers from the East were enthralled and invested in the prospects available in the West. One of these investors was Thomas A. Edison, who came to Dolores in 1900 to build a large plant to test out his new "secret" method of extracting gold from ore using static electricity. Even after several attempts, spending large amounts of money, this process proved to be unsuccessful. Edison would then move on to other endeavors. Today, the town's former general store and saloon serve as headquarters for a private ranch and are not accessible to the public.

GOLDEN

35.26699, -106.21391

Established in 1879, the gold mining town of Golden was preceded by El Real de San Francisco and Placer del Tuerto when the yellow metal was discovered in the 1820s. Even though gold fever hit a peak in 1825, when gold was discovered on the southwest slopes of the Ortiz Mountains, this valley remained quiet until it caught the interest of large mining outfits. Golden was the unofficial center of the gold mining communities and gold rush in New Mexico, with its expansive gold placer fields and mills on the northern slopes of the San Pedro Mountains. Golden expanded enough to welcome a school, mine support businesses, a stock exchange and, of course, several well-used saloons. The town's post office would open in 1880, only to close in 1928.

San Francisco Catholic Church was built there in 1830 to serve as a place of worship for the mining camps and surrounding communities. Constructed from adobe brick covered in plaster, San Francisco is one of the most photographed churches along the Turquoise Trail. A gravel trail wanders through the graveyard, which features weathered wooden and concrete crosses of parishioners, sometimes protected by wooden or iron fences. A child's white metal bedframe placed lovingly over a small grave is especially heartbreaking. Some of the wooden grave markers have all but succumbed to the elements—so much so that only God knows who is buried there.

Famed historian, author and Franciscan friar Angelico Chavez—who has a history and photography library in downtown Santa Fe named in his honor—lovingly restored the quaint church when time had started to take its toll in the 1960s. As an author of short stories, novels and poetry, Chavez, a twelfth-generation New Mexican born in Wagon Mound, was appointed the archivist for the Archdiocese of Santa Fe, where he took on the daunting task of translating and cataloging the extensive collection of Spanish archives stored in the state capitol.

During this time, the priest reevaluated the history he had been taught and began writing on these revelations. Many considered him a revisionist, mostly due to his opposing view of the Pueblo Revolt of 1680. He gained this view from research he obtained from previously undiscovered genealogical records. These minimized the role played by Native leader Po'pay in the revolution and created controversy. This view could have been one of the

Left: A highly photographed church in Golden, New Mexico.

Below: Remnants of mine operations and a schoolhouse.

Opposite: Dilapidated houses are all that remain in the once-thriving mining town.

reasons Chavez left the priesthood in 1971, after a crisis of faith, only to return to the priesthood in 1989. After his death in 1996, Chavez was buried in the Rosario Cemetery in Santa Fe.

A more recent preservation of the beautiful church has been taken on by members of the Montaño family, who have several generations of family members buried in the small graveyard. Mass is still held there every Saturday for the locals. The serene setting of the mission church draws many to the church grounds to reflect and take stunning photographs.

As the gold dwindled, so did the population in Golden, as they felt the pains of decreasing livelihoods. One surviving pioneer business is still open today. The Golden General Merchandise Store, now known as Henderson General Store, has been owned by the same family since 1918. Opened by Ernest and Lucy Riccon, the store was a vital source of daily items for those along the Turquoise Trail. In 1926, Vera, the Riccon's youngest daughter, purchased the store from her retiring parents, and she and her husband, Bill Henderson, continued to run the store until Vera's death in 2009 and Bill's death in 2015. The store was then taken over by their daughter and son-in-law, Desiri and Allen Henderson, who continue the tradition of running the store. The Henderson General Store is home to countless examples of fine Native and southwestern pieces of art, including pottery, rugs, jewelry and Kachina dolls.

The few occupied homes in Golden are surrounded by the derelicts of the past—abandoned company houses and mineshafts. Vandalism has claimed anything of value from the town while leaving marks behind in the form of graffiti. The town is located ten miles south of Madrid and fifteen miles north of Tijeras on NM-14.

Madrid

35.4067, -106.15252

Known as one of the quirkiest towns in New Mexico, Madrid (pronounced MAD-rid) has made a name for itself over the years as the "town too high to die." Narrow NM-14, which runs through the mountain hamlet, is generally lined with cars, recreational vehicles and motorcycles on any given day, as visitors flock to shop in the town's unique stores, which feature work from the many talented local artists who now call Madrid their home.

This tiny village has also made a name for itself in the film industry, as it was used as the setting of many movies, starting in 1970 with *The McMaster's* and continuing to 2007 with *Wild Hogs*, starring Tim Allen, John Travolta, Martin Lawrence, William H. Macy, Ray Liotta and Marisa Tomei, and *Conspiracy*, starring Val Kilmer and Gary Cole. Most recently, it has been the setting for *Beer for My Horses*, a 2008 comedy starring country singer Toby Keith.

Another interesting historical feature of Madrid, aside from its forty quirky shops and Bohemian vibes, is that it used to be known for its over-the-top Christmas light displays, especially in the 1920s and 1930s. So spectacular and bright were the lights that airlines would vary their routes a bit to show passengers the sight. Participation in parades, light displays, and celebrations were mandatory for residency in the tiny town, as miners were required to purchase a tree for light displays. One perk was that the electric plant was owned by the mining company and provided free electricity to the town at Christmastime.

What ghost town book would be complete without a few ghost stories? Madrid certainly has a few to tell. The Mine Shaft Tavern at the southern end of the town has been a longtime landmark. Many generations of miners, residents and visitors have enjoyed the atmosphere of the saloon, which is said to have the longest bar in New Mexico at a length of forty feet. Some enjoyed the tavern so much, they never left. Mine Shaft Tavern staff report

Madrid is now a unique artist colony.

Madrid has a thriving tourist trade.

Popular Mine Shaft Tavern is reportedly haunted.

witnessing glasses fall from shelves unassisted, as well as doors swinging open and shut without anyone around and noises emanating from the adobe walls that sound like voices and furniture being moved around. A ghostly image of a cowboy escorting a beautiful woman down Main Street has been widely reported. But the most disturbing of all accounts is the mirror that when peered into shows not the reflection of the person but a haunting ghostly image. Madrid embraces its dead, as the residents routinely have parties at the unique graveyard, named the Land of the Dead, in honor of their passed loved ones.

The original Mine Shaft Tavern burned down on Christmas Day in 1944, but it was lovingly rebuilt and restored by Oscar Huber in 1947. Today's tavern has been open since 1947, although the renovations were not completed until 1982. The Mine Shaft Tavern continues to be a lively spot to eat, drink, listen to live music and people watch. Art Colony Madrid attracts a variety of visitors from all walks of life. Creativity, as well as inspiration, is everywhere you look in Madrid, as many of the miners' shacks have been converted into brightly painted art studios. The word *eclectic* comes to mind when describing this historic mining town that also served as the terminus of the Santa Fe Branch Line from Waldo in 1906.

OTOWI

35.87586, -106.14252

Meaning "the gap where the water sinks" in the Tewa language, *Otowi* (pronounced OH-toe-ee) or *Potsuwi'i* is located on the north side of Pueblo Canyon, near modern-day Los Alamos, New Mexico. It includes a twenty-nine-acre historic district, including the Otowi Suspension Bridge. This bridge, which spans the Rio Grande seven miles west of San Ildefonso Pueblo, was built in 1924 and remains the only public highway suspension bridge in the state. Measuring 194 feet across and 10 feet wide, the timber bridge is an engineering marvel and was used to transport materials to Los Alamos for the development of the atomic bomb. Otowi Suspension Bridge was, in all reality, a link between the ancient cultures of the Pueblo and the nuclear world.

The bridge's location has been significant since ancient times, when the San Ildefonso Pueblo called it the *Poh-Sah-Con-Gay*, translated as the "place when the river makes noise." In 1886, the Rio Grande was spanned in this spot by the Denver and Rio Grande Western Railroad on a steel trestle bridge, which was used much later as an automobile bridge. Multiple floods washed out piers and abutments over the years, so a suspension design was introduced to alleviate this problem, allowing the bridge to be utilized until 1974. Otowi Suspension Bridge was put in the National Register of Historic Places for Santa Fe County in 1997. Today, the Otowi Suspension Bridge is visible and accessible from NM-502.

SAN PEDRO

35.2397, -106.2111

The gold strike of 1846 fueled the addition of the town of San Pedro, which, with four hundred residents, built a general store, three saloons and a hotel. A large copper mine, established in 1835, was operated about two miles away from the town by the Santa Fe Gold and Copper Company, which drew more miners to the area for work. There were also two mines operated by the San Pedro and Cañon de Agua Company near the town. A dispute with the Santa Fe Gold and Copper Company over mineral rights ended with a few of San Pedro's most influential residents behind bars after they attempted to seize property from the company.

It was a lack of water and the land litigation that put an end to San Pedro's copper mining in 1887, but gold was found by Thomas Wright, who opened the Lucky Mine and Smelter. This discovery sparked new life for the community, as businesses began to return. The court ruled against Wright's company over mineral rights in 1888, so he was bought out by the Lewisohn family in 1889, who operated the Santa Fe Gold and Copper Company until World War I.

W.S. Carnahan operated some of the mines throughout the 1920s and 1930s, when a post office was also established there. But with the Great Depression, drought, the drop in copper prices, et cetera, the town was short-lived, and the only remains of the once-prosperous community are a few ruins of coke ovens, building foundations and a lonely cemetery.

2
BERNALILLO COUNTY

Juan Tomas

35.02699, -106.29836

Located in the foothills of the Manzanita Mountains, this village is home to the area's farmers and loggers. The original town was abandoned in the mid-1960s due to a lack of water. One of the most beautiful remnants of that era is the over one-hundred-year-old Juan Tomas Church, which is located private land on NM-217, south of old Route 66, at Juan Tomas Road, but it can be enjoyed from the gate. This church and one residence have been restored and are still being used today, but it is not used for Catholic services, since it was sold by the Archdiocese of Santa Fe to a private owner. Approximately two miles west of the church on Highway 217 is the rarely used Juan Tomas Cemetery with all Hispanic names recorded.

The town was named for ranch owner John Thomas in 1870. It is reported that pinto beans were the main crop grown by the community, and sawmills were in the village in the late nineteenth century. As part of the Cañon de Carnuel Land Grant, many of the townsmen worked the mines in Golden, Madrid and San Pedro.

Please be advised, this region gets a large amount of snow in the winter months, so it is recommended you plan your trip for the milder months, from May to November. For those of you who enjoy hiking, the 3.7-mile-long

Juan Tomas Open Space Loop is one of the best hiking experiences in New Mexico for beginners, mountain bikers and families—even the pups can tag along if you keep them on a leash.

Paa-ko

35.1019905, -106.3778019

Paa-ko, which means, "root of the cottonwood tree," is home to numerous stacked rock ruins of an ancient Tiwa settlement, many reaching up to two stories and dating to about 1200 CE, but they were abandoned by 1670. The earliest known documentation of the site is from the writings of Adolph Bandelier, who described the pueblo in his report from 1892. At the pueblo's peak, it contained hundreds of rooms, with a historic plaza being added in the 1600s, after the Spanish Entrada.

Evidence of metallurgy was found at Paa-ko, which indicates the Pueblo people and Spaniards were creating items and jewelry from the abundant ores found around their home. Copper sheeting, iron scale and lead ore was found in the plaza area, where a smelting feature was found. Paa-ko is thought to have been a part of the eleven Magua Pueblos, which include nearby Tajique, Quarai, Chilili, Abo and Gran Quivira.

Called a large classic ancestral pueblo with both circular and square kivas, Paa-ko is located west of San Pedro Creek in the San Pedro Valley, east of the majestic Sandia Mountains. Paa-ko is eight miles north of the town of Tijeras, close to the ghost town of Golden and is easily accessible. It was commissioned as a New Mexico State Monument in 1938 but was decommissioned in 1959. The number of ruins has been dramatically reduced due to erosion and souvenir hunters, but the pueblo is used as an archaeology dig site and is owned by the University of New Mexico. These ruins are fascinating to explore, but remember, it is illegal to remove any items, including rocks, from archaeological sites.

3

TORRANCE COUNTY

CEDARVALE

34.37062, -105.70195

Pinto beans were king in central New Mexico during the 1920s. Cedarvale, along with Claunch and Mountainair, were large producers of the legume. Established in 1908, the site of Cedarvale was chosen because it was along the route of the New Mexico Central Railroad—vitally important for shipping. Founders William Taylor, Oliver P. DeWolfe and Ed Smith sold lots for development and named their new town Cedarvale after the Kansas town of the same name they were from.

The location attracted up to five hundred residents, who arrived on the "immigrant trains," and a post office was opened. Pinto beans did exceptionally well in the area's high altitude, which was great for the American soldiers abroad for whom the crops were grown. When the Great Depression, the Dust Bowl and droughts hit the state, it was difficult to keep the crops growing, so many moved on to better prospects. The post office closed recently in 1990, and only a few residents remain in Cedarvale.

One of the most impressive buildings in the town is the derelict remains of the school. Finished by the Works Progress Administration (WPA) in 1921 at a cost of $5,000, the school housed children from kindergarten to eighth grade. The massive gymnasium was used for community events, as well as sporting events for the school, which used the structure's wooden

Above: Rattlesnake warnings and ruins go together in Cedarvale.

Left: Cedarvale School is an impressive ruin.

Opposite: Stone lions guard what is left of what was once a beautiful rock home.

backboards for basketball and a stage for plays. After closing in 1953, the Cedarvale School's sturdy construction stood the test of time until recently. Old desks can still be found adorning the rooms, and chalkboards still have some of the lessons visible under the graffiti, but the roof has long since collapsed, making a journey inside the building perilous. Also, be aware of the rattlesnakes that have reportedly taken up residence there, as there are no nearby hospitals available. The outhouse in the back is a step back in time for sure.

Today, the town is just a blink on Highway 42 to Willard, New Mexico, but the interesting architecture of several of the remaining homes is a diversion worth the side trip.

ENCINO

34.65118, -105.46167

Situated on U.S.-285, between the towns of Vaughn and Clines Corners, New Mexico, Encino is a quick "don't blink or you'll miss it" town that has very few modern amenities aside from the post office and bunch of derelict buildings—a photographer's dream. Meaning "oak" in Spanish, Encino has certainly stood true as an oak, but it was named for the scrub oaks found on the landscape around the town.

Bonnie Salas is given credit for being the first homesteader in Encino, but prior to her arrival, Encino was used by travelers as a rest stop, as a fresh spring was in the area. Most of the residents were sheep or cattle ranchers. In 1905, the railroad started making plans to build a depot in the tiny village,

This derelict house in Encino has seen better days.

An old storefront in Encino is slowly crumbling with time.

and Bonnie Salas sold forty acres of land to the Bond family, who then sold it to the Atchison, Topeka and Santa Fe Railroad to build a depot. The B.G. Bond Mercantile was built there in 1905, and it doubled as the depot for a short time. This was the only store in Encino until 1908, when A.R. Cecil established his lumber business in 1908.

One of the best-known persons from Encino was R.C. Dillion, the eighth governor of New Mexico who served two terms. In the 1920s, Encino was a stop along the unpaved Highway 60. Even with Governor Dillion's influence, much of Highway 60 remained unpaved until the 1950s. In 1965, the train depot closed, and in 1982, the high school closed its doors as well. At one time, the gymnasium of the high school contained southwestern murals by artist Hallie Williams, which she painted for twenty dollars between 1939 and 1942. Unfortunately, many of these murals are now gone. A little trip off the main Highway 285 will be a step back in time. Be sure to have your camera ready, as I'm sure you will be itching to snap plenty of images—but hurry, the buildings are fading away quickly.

Manzano

34.64673, -106.34502

Land in the Manzano region has been planted with apple orchards since the 1600s, so Manzano (which means apple in Spanish) has the proud distinction of having the oldest apple orchards in the United States, with some having been planted before 1676. Be on the lookout for descendants of these trees scattered along the sides of the highway. The original settlement was an ancient pueblo, part of the nearby Salinas Missions of Abo, Gran Quivira and Quarai. The official start date of the town of Manzano was November 28, 1829, when the Spanish established a settlement there.

As one of the stops on the winding scenic route between NM-33 and NM-55 and on to U.S.-60 from Tijeras, New Mexico, Manzano immediately takes you back to simpler, peaceful times as it sports a population of a little over fifty-four residents. You may encounter a cyclist utilizing the bike lane, so use caution when navigating the narrow switchbacks of the mountainous portion of the trip. The tiny village of approximately forty souls features a quaint Catholic church with a well-tended graveyard in front. Manzano is welcoming to visitors and photographers, with colorful murals painted on its vintage adobe buildings. East of town is a lake that features a torreon, or defense tower, that was built to defend the town from the frequent attacks of the Native tribes.

This mural in Montano celebrates the rural way of life.

NEGRA

34.66396, -105.53723

A former service station is the first structure of the town of Negra you will see as you travel along U.S.-60, five miles from Encino. From a distance, it looks like any other concrete and plaster construction from the 1940s or 1950s, but on closer inspection, you will see the subtle details that reveal its true age. Floral-patterend pressed-tin ceiling tiles and Greco design edgings not only adorn the interior of the small, plastered building but also are featured underneath the defunct drive-through portico. The elements have aged this beauty well with just the right amount of rusty gold and patina. Inside the building, which sports a "U.S. Post Office" sign painted on the outside (although this building was never used as a post office—it was just built by the postmaster), sit three dusty church pews and two rather well-preserved ovens from the 1920s.

Negra's post office was established in 1909 but would see its demise only nine years later in 1918. The residents would then have to travel a short distance to Encino to retrieve their mail. Along with many of the neighboring towns around it, Negra was established when the Belen Cutoff was constructed by the Atchison, Topeka and Santa Fe Railroad and opened in 1907 to cut a two-hundred-plus-mile-long main line across the plains of eastern New Mexico and the northern Texas Panhandle to divert most of the railroad's transcontinental traffic off the Raton Pass Line. This cutoff spurred significant economic and population growth along the route and is still used as the Southern Transcon of the Burlington Northern, and Santa Fe Railroad today. The heavy locomotives of the Burlington, Northern and Santa Fe Railroad still rumble by the sleepy town, and one can only imagine what life was like living along the railway in a desolate part of the state.

A little farther up the road from the service station sits a magnificent old rock house adorned with an enclosed glass-paneled porch. This home belonged to Hallie Williams and her husband, Albert "Ollie." Hallie was the mural artist in the previous segment about Encino. Ollie ran the filling station and the mercantile store along the railroad track in Encino. There were a total of three stores owned by Ollie—not to mention a small herd of American bison.

There are a couple of stories about how Negra (Spanish for "black") received its name. One is an urban legend that says the town was named

The gas station that doubled as a post office is now storage for church pews.

A tourist motor court once provided shelter for travelers.

for a black dog that was living in the town at the time. The other—and probably more likely account—comes from author Robert Julyan's book *The Place Names of New Mexico*, which states the town was built on rich, black soil and that there was a black water tank on the property as well. Despite its name, Negra's water was good-tasting and abundant, as it would be used as the water source for Encino and Duran.

PIÑOS WELLS

34.44590, -105.62861

A lonely cemetery and a few rock walls are all that remain of Piños Wells, which was founded in 1895 with twenty-one residents as a stage stop between Santa Fe/Las Vegas and White Oaks, New Mexico. On the plains, nearly in the dead center of New Mexico, Piños Wells lies south of Pino Mountain, surrounded by numerous cattle ranches. The town got its name by the existence of two wells surrounded by a couple of pine trees in the area. The stage stop provided food, water and lodging for U.S. House of Representatives member Jose Francisco Chaves, who served the New Mexico Territory At-Large District from 1865 to 1867. He was a rancher in Piños Wells and gained a tragic claim to fame when he was assassinated by a shooter while eating dinner at the home of a friend on November 26, 1904.

Chaves's daughter, Dolores Elizabeth "Lola" Chavez de Armijo, was the state's librarian but faced opposition when Governor William McDonald fought to remove her in 1912, stating that women were not qualified to hold this position under the constitution and laws of New Mexico. It is also thought McDonald was intending to put a close friend of his in the position and that Armijo stood in the way. Armijo was successful in keeping her position after the New Mexico Supreme Court ruled in her favor and implemented legislature allowing women to hold appointed office in New Mexico. Armijo is honored with a New Mexico Historic Women Marker near Albuquerque for her contribution to the advancement of women in the state. On a side note: McDonald, who was New Mexico State's first governor, was buried in an unassuming grave in the nearby cemetery of White Oaks, located on County Road C014, north of Highway 54, between Encino and Corona.

PART II

NORTHEAST NEW MEXICO

4

TAOS COUNTY

LA BELLE

36.7628079, -105.305591

After the discovery of gold and development of the Edison Mine in 1894 by Ira Wing, the mining towns began popping up quickly. La Belle was formed approximately eight miles northeast of Red River when hundreds of prospectors and gold miners descended on Comanche Creek in the Carson National Forest around 1896. At this time, the land was part of the Sangre de Cristo Land Grant and was owned by the Freehold Land and Emigration Company, a Dutch company.

So many mining claims were staked in the area that the Keystone Mining District was formed. Due to the district being located on the private land of Freehold, extra fees were charged to the miners to utilize the claims. This caused miners to move westward, a few miles to Bitter Creek.

If any of you are fans of the series *Godless*, you will be interested to know it is filmed in and loosely based on the real-life town of La Belle. Situated at the base of Van Diest Mountain in an expansive valley, La Belle was reportedly named after Belle Dixon, the wife of one of the founders of the camp. Between the years 1894 and 1895, the population of the town had grown to over six hundred. It is reported that the ratio between women and men in the town was hugely disproportionate, with possibly only fifteen eligible women living the mining town. In fact, there were so few women in the town, the town's men would travel fifty miles to Catskill to attend its fandangos.

As with other boom towns, La Belle featured three saloons, which were said to have been frequented by outlaws. One train robber in particular, Tom "Black Jack" Ketchum, as well as his brother Sam, was said to truly enjoy the dances that were held at the Nadock Hotel, one of the towns three hotels. Bert and Frank Akers opened their saloon, the Musician's Headquarters, which had a fancy ring to it, but the second story of the establishment was used by the many prostitutes who worked there, with some of the women brought in from Colorado Springs.

The Musician's Headquarters also made a name for itself as the site of many raucous nights and as a place that served Taos Lightning, a spicy brand of whiskey that was said to have been developed by mountain man Peg-Leg Smith and his partners in 1824. (Other tales have said a Kentucky-born Taos distiller, Simeon Turley, originally produced the wheat-based rot gut in 1830.) The trappers claimed the concoction was strong enough to "grow hair on the hide of a Chihuahua and make one feel like he had been struck by lightning," which is not surprising, since the whiskey was reportedly forty to fifty proof. Customers would get so rowdy with this drink that saloon owners in Missouri were known to lace the liquor with laudanum to calm them down.

According to New Mexico historian Marc Simmons, the Taos Lightning recipes read like this: to one gallon of silty water from the Rio Grande, add a pint of raw grain alcohol, a dash of bitters, a pinch of Jamaican ginger and a plug of chewing tobacco (no indication if this was fresh or chewed). Stir the mixture and age overnight. It has also been described as barbarous an alcoholic compound ever made. The whiskey even made it into episode six, season three of the original *Star Trek*, an episode titled "Spectre of the Gun."

The Southern Hotel boasted four stories and eighty rooms; moved from Catskill, the Exchange Hotel was a smaller fourteen-room hotel operated by the Nadocks, which also doubled as an official stage stop and another unnamed hotel. The Nadocks' daughter, Annie, was said to be frequent dance partner of Tom "Black Jack" Ketchum at her parents property. Local legend states that Ketchum buried a cache of several thousand dollars in the Le Belle area, but sadly, it has never been located.

To keep up with the demand from the population, five general stores, a newspaper, two barbershops, two laundries, a jail and four livery barns were quickly added to the small mountain hamlet. In total, there were eighty buildings in La Belle during its heyday. All was good and promising for the town until 1910, when the gold ore was deemed low-grade, causing all but ten miners to leave the town. La Belle steadily declined into oblivion.

MIDNIGHT/ANCHOR

36.7639, -105.3528

The Midnight Mining Camp, founded by M.K. Long and two partners, is located four miles northwest of Red River, New Mexico, and half a mile west of the town of Anchor. Sitting atop the stunningly beautiful Cimarron Ridge at 9,600 feet are the remains of log cabins that were crudely built to house the influx of gold miners flooding into northern New Mexico. Established in 1895, the Midnight Mining Camp also encompassed the towns of Midnight, Memphis, Caribel, Edison and Anchor. Known today as Midnight Meadows, the remnants of the mining operation still stand true as a testament of determination in the Carson National Forest.

The gold ore found in the area along Bitter Creek sustained these communities for approximately three years—well into 1898—with a population of over two hundred. But it is recorded that the lack of free-milling ores and land litigations forced the abandonment of these towns. According to historians James and Barbara Sherman, the decision of abandonment of the Midnight Mine came so quickly that the shells of thirty-two hand-hewn log cabins that were under construction were left unfinished. Legend has it that the name Midnight came about because the trees were so tall that the sun did not reach the ground. Midnight was also thought to have been on the route of the Pony Express, and in the 1950s, the Silver Dollar Saloon was still standing—named after the silver dollars imbedded in the bar.

The services available to the mining towns were the Ellis and Co. General Merchandise Store, Hays and Co. Blacksmith and a justice of the peace. Mail and passenger stages ran an average of three times a week from the town of Catskill, which was fifty-eight miles away. The gold and silver mined in the four local mines was sent to Denver, Colorado, for processing.

The Midnight Mine was originally owned by the Dutch investment group Freehold Land and Emigration Company, which purchased the promising land from the Costilla Estate, located in the southern half of the Sangre de Cristo Land Grant.

Twining

36.59475, -105.45028

Originally known as Amizette, a New Jersey bank president, Albert C. Twining, helped finance the Frazer Copper Company by lending it over $22,000. With this kind of backing, the town was named in his honor in 1900. Soon, the village began to suffer a series of hard-luck situations, which threatened to destroy Twining before it was able to establish itself.

In 1903, Albert C. Twining was tried and convicted for fraud and sent to prison for the embezzlement of, initially, over $12,000 from the Asbury Park Bank in New Jersey, where he was formerly employed. According to case records, Twining used most of the Monmouth Trust and Safe Deposit and the First National Bank's money to travel to New Mexico to purchase $90,000 worth of shares in the Fraser Copper Company Mine. Once revealed, these actions spurred a panic run—even with the reassurance of Twining—with investors eventually forcing the bank to shut its doors and go into receivership. Good news for the depositors: 97 percent of their deposits were returned. Unfortunately, many underhanded deals reportedly done by Twining rendered the bank's shares worthless.

Once Albert Twining was out of the picture, prospector William Fraser staked numerous claims along the Rio Hondo District at the encouragement of mining brothers Alex and William Anderson in 1877. In Fraser's efforts, he was able to discover enough ore and placer gold to become the most renowned prospector and mine trader in the Taos Valley. By the summer of 1883, Fraser had sold sixteen full claims and three-quarter interest in seven others, all while continuing his mining operations. Fraser then partnered with Jack Bidwell and Clarence Probert of the Taos Bank to begin mining again. Unfortunately, when you deal with money and valuable commodities, mistrust can creep in. Jack Bidwell accused William Fraser of stealing the investment money. A heated argument ensued, which resulted in the shooting death of Fraser at Bidwell's hands. This was literally the nail in the town of Twining's coffin.

Mining shacks were moved to Taos, and the mill burned down in 1932, erasing what little remained of the town. Today, Twining is now part of the Taos Ski Resort, but only pieces of broken concrete and rusted pipes can still be seen if you have an eagle eye.

5

COLFAX COUNTY

BALDY

36.6292, -105.2139

Near the top of Baldy Mountain, which has an elevation of 12,446 feet, the town of Baldy was established and was known for its placer gold and copper deposits. Attention was drawn to the region when the Utes began to mine in the area around 1866. These mines included the Mystic Lode Copper Mine and the Aztec, French Henry, Bull-of-the-Woods and the Black Horse Mines. These mines—and seven more—stretched for seventy miles along the mountain and produced $4 million worth of gold during their heyday.

The population steadily grew to two hundred by 1897, when a Methodist church, school, blacksmith shop, barbershop, livery stable, laundry a justice of the peace and, naturally, many saloons lined the dirt roads of the town. Baldy was one of the few towns to have a telegraph line as well.

By 1900, prospectors gathered in the area, following rumors of a hidden gold mother lode. W.P. McIntyre was so convinced that the treasured metal was located two thousand feet inside the tall peak that he began a thirty-six-year-long project of drilling a tunnel through Baldy Mountain—starting on each side and meeting in the middle. Unfortunately for McIntyre, he passed away in 1930, before the tunnel was complete. This tunnel project was never finished, although the tunnels were reportedly drilled within an inch of each other. But the legendary mother lode remained elusive. The town of Baldy would limp along, mining copper and gold until 1941, when the buildings were razed.

In 1963, 10,098 acres of the mountain property was bought and donated to the Philmont Boy Scout Ranch near Cimarron, New Mexico, by Norton Clapp. The property is now located on the northwestern border of the ranch. In a recent forest fire, some of the remaining structures, smelter slag pile, tailing pile and foundations of the gravity-fed mill used in Baldy were scorched.

CATSKILL

36.9475, -104.8075

It is interesting to note that Catskill, established 1892, was reported to be one of the few ghost towns in New Mexico without a tragic past. As a charcoal producer, Catskill was known to burn three thousand cords of wood each day in its ten coke ovens. These ovens were used to convert the bituminous coal, which was mined in the area, into industrial coke, which is a clean-burning fuel used in the process of smelting iron ore.

Descriptions of Catskill sketch a story of the perfect western town—without violence. Citizens worked together to build a church, a recreation hall, a ballpark, a racetrack and even a dance hall, where the town's twenty-two-piece band and a dance orchestra played. Although, as life goes, Catskill was not without its drama. In July 1896, a devastating flood destroyed the Catskill branch of the Union Pacific, Denver and Gulf Railroad, which was forty miles long, running from Trinidad, Colorado, to the Maxwell Land Grant in New Mexico. The destruction of the railway was so complete that a new survey was done to make a new route. When it was built, the Union Pacific Line stretched from Catskill to Elizabethtown and Cimarron, through the Mora Valley, Las Vegas, White Oaks and finally into El Paso, Texas.

Along with the coke ovens, the town was home to up to six sawmills that utilized the lumber around the town, which was set twenty miles southwest of the Colorado border and thirty-five miles west of Raton, New Mexico. In the town's heyday, thirty to fifty railcars of lumber were shipped from Catskill daily. Due to this demand, lumber became scarce by 1902, and the sawmills began to close shop. The final demise of the town was ultimately the decision by the Colorado and Southern Railway to pull up its tracks from Catskill.

Remains of the twenty-five redbrick coke ovens that surrounded the town are almost all that is left of Catskill today. Each charcoal oven measures twenty-eight feet tall and featured two six-foot-tall arched openings and walls that are fifteen feet thick. Since the village, now in the National Register of Historic Places, was a railway town, the roads to and from it are accessible, but it is highly recommended that you travel in a high-clearance, four-wheel-drive vehicle. It is a hard drive, not good on tires, so be prepared if you decide to venture in.

CLIFTON (CLIFTON HOUSE)

36.8158597, -104.4544318

All that remains of this cattle town are the wooden grave markers in its small cemetery. Built in 1867 by cattleman Tom Stockton as headquarters for his large cattle roundup, Clifton House was also an overnight stop on the Barlow-Sanderson Stage Line. The materials used to build this structure were brought over land from Dodge City, Kansas. Luckily for Clifton, Barlow-Sanderson Stage Lines built a blacksmith shop and stables in the town to service the stage as it came through; it also employed cooks and waiters to help the passengers during their stays.

This stage line originated from Missouri and traveled farther and farther west as the line expanded. There were three classes of travelers on the stage: first class rode the stage the entire trip, second class had to get out and walk the more difficult stretches of road and the third class had to not only get out and walk, but they also had to help push the stage up the higher hills. Although the stagecoaches (fully loaded with passengers and luggage) weighed in at over a ton, generally only four horses were used to pull for the average 120 miles per day.

Clifton House, which was considered a fine inn during its heyday, featured a trading post and a post office by the early 1870s and was briefly counted as the headquarters for the English company that purchased the famed Maxwell Land Grant from Lucien B. Maxwell in 1870. Constructed using adobe, the two-story building contained a raised half-story basement, a three-sided veranda supported by Doric posts and a second-story balcony. Washbasins were in the front hall, and some of the rooms were graced with fireplaces.

Nothing was left of Clifton House after the fire but this marker.

In true Wild West tradition, Clifton House was also the site of a gunfight between the dangerous outlaw Robert "Clay" Allison and gunman Chunk Colbert. The incident occurred on January 7, 1874, while the two men were eating dinner at the high-ceilinged Clifton House after participating in a horse race. The men had a rocky past, as Allison had beaten Colbert's uncle years earlier for overcharging him and his family to cross the Brazos River in Texas. Apparently not over the past altercation, Colbert attempted to pull his pistol on Allison, but as luck would have it, the barrel became snagged, and Colbert was unable to complete his draw. Clay Allison was an exceptional gunman, so he was able to shoot Colbert in the head, killing him at the table. Later, when asked by the sheriff why he had accepted an invitation to dinner by a man who would try to kill him, Allison responded, "Because I didn't want to send a man to hell on an empty stomach."

When the Atchison, Topeka and Santa Fe Railroad arrived at Clifton in March 1879, it spelled the end for the Clifton House, which was abandoned. Unfortunately, the remaining building was destroyed by an arsonist fire in 1885. A historical marker is all that remains to remind the world of the Clifton House's existence.

COLMOR

36.22059, -104.64943

Along the steel rails that connect Colfax County to Mora County lies the forgotten town of Colmor, which is a combination of Colfax and Mora, since it straddles the county line. Partially fallen adobe and wooden buildings are located within fifty yards of the railway, giving passersby a glimpse into what the railroad town might have looked like when it was settled in 1887. As the supply hub for surrounding ranches, Colmor had a couple of stores, a library, a gas station, a school and the Brown Hotel.

In anticipation of the arrival of the Colmor Cutoff as a companion to the Belen Cutoff, the town was expecting great things to come its way after an agricultural report in 1925 sang the praises of the town's potential. In 1929, the construction of the Colmor Cutoff began but only saw twenty-six of the proposed fifty-eight miles completed before the onslaught of the Great Depression in 1931. Since there was no need for passenger trains during the World Wars, the tracks were pulled, and the steel allocated to the war efforts in 1942. Colmor Cutoff was not to be.

Colmor is one of the few ghost towns in this volume that listed a library as one of its buildings. Although this was an unconventional type of building—a boxcar—it was a library, nonetheless. The Literary Club of Colmor bought a boxcar for ten dollars and transformed it into a public library. To raise funds to remodel the boxcar, each citizen was given an envelope so they could contribute to the project. A message in the envelope read, "The Colmor Library needs a mile of pennies. Sixteen pennies make one foot. Please place one foot or more in the envelope." At the dedication in 1929, 31 books were donated to start the library's collection; by 1932, there were 1,200 books available at the library. Ultimately, the library's collection included 3,500 books, which is amazing for a library serving a population of seventy-five residents.

The boxcar library, books and all, was later sold to the Caldwell's in nearby Springer. Colmor also sported a public school, which unfortunately burned to the ground since the town did not have a fire station. The next year, however, a new, brick and stone school was erected at a cost of $13,000 in 1919. This building is now the largest ruin on the townsite.

Luck did not visit Colmor, as the town was bypassed by Highway 85, which spanned between Springer and Wagon Mound, New Mexico. Others who have visited the town give a warning about the possibility of rattlesnakes being its only residents today. Please be careful—make plenty of noise, carry a walking stick and maybe invest in a good pair of snake guards as you explore the remnants of Colmor. You must go through a gate to access the town; it is imperative that you close this gate as you enter and exit. This is still ranchland. If you take Exit 404 from I-25, turn right once you cross the railroad tracks at the intersection—do not go straight, as this is a private ranch. There are no signs to direct you to Colmor from the interstate other than the exit, and it can be confusing.

Dawson

36.6641997, -104.7747179

According to online accounts and other published personal accounts, Dawson is widely known as the most haunted ghost town in New Mexico. Due to the amount of tragedy that occurred in the small mining town, that assessment is most likely correct. A lonely cemetery filled with over 382 white metal crosses is the town's most prominent feature. These crosses represent the number of miners who lost their lives in the mine explosions of October 22, 1913, killing 261 men, and February 28, 1923, which killed 121 more. These explosions were strong enough that they were said to have physically shaken Dawson.

When John Barkley Dawson settled in the Vermejo River Valley in 1869, he had no idea how large his tiny town would grow between 1901 and 1950. With a population that varied between two thousand and nine thousand, Dawson was one of the largest mining operations in New Mexico. It was born when the Dawson to Tucumcari line of the railroad was constructed. Soon, the mining town sported a hotel, theater, newspaper, baseball park, golf course, bowling alley and hospital, which was basically unheard of in the early 1900s in New Mexico. In the 1950s, Phelps Dodge sold the entire town lock, stock and barrel, leaving only the cemetery behind.

Today, the town's cemetery and remnants of the town are located on private property, but they can be seen past the corral fencing. To explore Dawson, travel seventeen miles east of Cimarron on U.S.-64 and A38, where you will see the graveyard.

Tragic mining disasters plagued Dawson.

Elizabethtown

36.6192, -105.28445

In the shade of Mount Baldy sits the remnants of a once-booming mining town known as Elizabethtown and the home of one of New Mexico's first serial killers: Charles Kennedy (Canady). From 1865 to 1870, Kennedy ran a rest stop along the Taos Trail to give weary travelers a place to relax before continuing their journey. Unfortunately, for over fourteen of his guests, their rest was permanent. His story reads much like that of the Bender family of Kansas, also known as the Bloody Benders, who lured people into their small cabin with the help of a pretty woman who promised food and a clean bed. Death was dealt by an iron skillet across the back of the diner's head. They would then be robbed of any valuables and either disposed of under the floorboards or in a shallow grave—whichever was more convenient at the time.

With Kennedy, he used his young wife, Gregoria, and young son, Samuel, to look normal, thwarting any suspicion by posing as a family man. Their guests would then be killed in their sleep, and once they were devoid of valuables, their bodies were burned or buried. This operation continued regularly until one of the visitors asked if there were any Natives in the area, to which his nine-year-old son at the time piped up, stating, "Can't you smell the one Papa put under the floor?" Enraged by his son's candidness, the young man met his death at his father's hands when his head was bashed into the stone fireplace. The visitor did not fare any better, as he met his fate with a bullet from Kennedy's pistol. Kennedy then put both bodies in the cellar, locked his hysterical wife in a room and drank himself into a stupor.

After escaping through the chimney, Gregoria walked close to fifteen miles to Elizabethtown to recount the horrors she had experienced. The young woman's tale enraged the townsfolk including Clay Allison, who went to the cabin and arrested Kennedy. Even though the evidence against Kennedy was immense, with charred remains and partial skeletons found in and around the cabin, due justice had to be administered. Rumors were flying that Kennedy's lawyer, Melvin W. Mills, was trying to buy his freedom, and this did not sit well with some in town—namely, gunslingers Clay Allison and Davy Crockett (grand-nephew of the famous frontiersman), who broke the killer out of the jail. Several accounts of what happened to the killer have been told, but none bode well for the accused.

The Mutz hotel is Elizabethtown's most distinctive landmark today. *Courtesy of the Library of Congress.*

One version says Allison, Crockett and other members of the town put a rope around Kennedy's neck and attached it to a horse, which dragged him through town until he lost his head. The other says his head was removed by Allison's ever-present Bowie knife. Either way, Kennedy did not survive and was beheaded. His body was buried outside the Catholic cemetery, but his head was rumored to have been used as a spike adornment outside of Lambert's Saloon (now the St. James Hotel) in Cimarron, some twenty-nine miles away. It was said to have been transported by gunny sack by Clay Allison, but this story has been questioned by numerous historians over the years. No matter the true story of his demise, Kennedy was thought to have killed more than one hundred men and two of his own children before his luck ran out.

Elizabethtown was founded by Captain William H. Moore, a commander of Fort Union who named the town after his daughter Elizabeth Catherine, the first schoolteacher in her namesake town. Although Elizabethtown started small, its population soon swelled to over seven thousand. It was nicknamed "E-Town" by the locals and became the county seat of Colfax County in 1870.

In what started as a copper mining town, legend tells of a Native who Captain Moore had found in gravely ill and nursed back to health at Fort Union returning to pay back the favor by bringing the captain some "pretty rocks." These rocks were found to have a high amount of copper. The captain was shown the upper slope of Baldy Mountain, where the rocks were found, and he staked a claim there immediately. While on this expedition, on a lark, the captain pulled out a gold pan to sift through some creek gravel and found gold. Copper was no longer the most important find of the day. The land where the discovery was made belonged to Lucien B. Maxwell, who began charging the men for use of his land. Each miner was allotted a five-hundred-square-foot area and paid one dollar a month to mine on it. Maxwell asked for twelve dollars in advance for placer or gulch claims, and he asked for half for the lode claims.

As the town began to flourish, it attracted many elements into its midst and by 1868 there were four hundred people living there. Many of those were residents of the red-light district who had a group of two-story cabins connected to the seven saloons. The ladies would use a dumb waiter to have drinks delivered to the rooms above for their clients.

Mining began to wane in 1872, but by 1875, when the Atchison, Topeka and Santa Fe Railroad advanced its track from Colorado into New Mexico, new life was breathed into the community. Dances were held often, which attracted the likes of people like outlaw Tom "Black Jack" Ketchum and his gang.

The Oro Dredging Company began to run its enormous dredge, which they named Eleanor and ran to handle up to four thousand cubic yards of pay dirt a day, through the mountain passes to Elizabethtown in 1901. It paid for itself when it recovered one-quarter of all the gold found in New Mexico that year. The Moreno Valley produced over $5 million worth of gold in seventy-five years. Operations in Elizabethtown were derailed by a devastating fire, which spread throughout the town, leaving only one store standing. Mining started to play out by 1917, and the town had perished by 1920.

Elizabethtown is approximately 4.8 miles north of Eagle Nest on NM-38. Turn left at the windmill and travel west onto the dirt road B-20 and

Elizabethtown was home to lawmen, outlaws and serial killers. *Courtesy of the Library of Congress.*

travel 0.3 miles to the turnoff. There are only a few buildings and three walls of the stone Mutz Hotel, which was tragically burned down by careless campers, remaining.

JOHNSON MESA/BELL

36.9120, -104.3289

One of the few remnants of Johnson Mesa is the stone St. John's Methodist Episcopal Church, which dates to 1897. The low mesa on the outskirts of the newly established town of Johnson Park gained its name from Johnson

Mesa in 1882. It was named for settler Elijah Johnson, who developed a cattle ranch on the mesa. Johnson grazed cattle on the mesa—a practice called *potreros* by the locals. Marion Bell, a rail worker, gathered a group of disgruntled and unemployed railroad workers and coal miners from the Raton area to begin homesteading in the Mesa area, but the settlement was centered on Lon Bell's home, so the group of houses was known as the town of Bell by 1887.

These homesteaders were granted 160 acres of free land under the Homestead Act of 1862, which allowed any American, including freed slaves, to claim up to 160 acres of federal land for a small filing fee. Due to this act, Johnson Mesa and Bell soon grew to a combined population of 487 by 1900. Volcanic soil on the mesa was a perfect growing source for hay, oats, a variety of vegetables and potatoes. The men of the town not only worked on the railroad and in coal mines, but they also worked in the fields. An ingenious carrier pigeon system was utilized by the mines to summon people from the fields to work when needed.

By 1910, the area's population dropped to 355, mainly due to the harsh winters, which were not conducive to farming. The influenza epidemic of 1918 reduced the area's population even further, to 215. Bell's post office closed in 1933, and by 1956, there were only 56 residents left in the area. Today, the only surviving reminders of the towns are the church and a small cemetery at Bell.

KOEHLER

36.74086, -104.61832

Coal was king in Colfax County, and this spurred the birth of many mining towns in the region, including Koehler (pronounced KAY-lor) in the early 1900s. Koehler was named for Henry Koehler, the president of the board of the American Brewing Company of St. Louis. Henry's brother Hugo was the vice-president of the Rock Mountain and Pacific Company, which owned the town. Located sixteen miles from Raton and the Colorado border, Koehler was said to boast a population of nearly 1,200—with people coming from all corners of the world to cash in on the area's fortune. This boom was maintained until 1924, when the railroads switched their engines to oil fuel from coal, which was the deathblow to many of the small coal mining towns in New Mexico.

In its boom days, Koehler was said to have a four- to six-foot-thick coal vein, which piqued miners' interests in 1898. As mining operations began, the construction of Koehler also began. A two-story school was built in 1905; a post office was added to the electric plant in 1907; and a doctor's office, three boardinghouses, a bathhouse, an amusement hall that was said to play movies and hold dances for the town and a one-hundred-foot-long saloon were also built. A company store was built alongside the railroad and provided all the provisions the town needed. At least 158 colorfully painted row houses were built to house the large number of miners flooding into the area. All the houses had electricity, and water was delivered by gravity from the reservoir that was built in 1908 on a hill above the town.

An astounding 210 coke ovens were built to produce 3,500 tons of coke a year as the company expanded into Waldron Canyon, west of the town. In 1923, tragedy struck the school, as a fire leveled it and the surrounding buildings (these buildings were never to be rebuilt). Also, in the same year, a miners' strike occurred and became so violent that over 600 soldiers sent to the town to keep peace. By 1924, the price of coal dropped so dramatically that the mines closed.

When the mines closed in 1924, Koehler officially became a ghost town, even though the post office operated in the town until 1932. But interest in the town would be renewed twelve years later, in 1936, when J. Van Houten (see the town of Van Houten) sought new leases in Koehler and installed new equipment, which was said to have cost $200,000. Unfortunately, since the mining operations did not start until 1940, the interest would not last long, and the town regained its ghost town status.

The Kaiser Steel Corporation purchased the property in 1955 but knocked down many of the structures that were still standing at that time. In 1957, the post office closed its doors for the last time. The Koehler Mine then experienced an electrical fire, which burned from June 1958 to October 1959.

What remains of Koehler are a few of the row houses; partial structures, such as the doctor's office, a shop and walls; partially complete coke ovens; and the foundation of the processing plant, which is now part of the Vermejo Park Ranch owned by Ted Turner, the largest landowner in the state. Accessibly to Koehler is now extremely limited, as the only people who can visit are the paying guests of the Vermejo Park Ranch.

RAYADO

36.3686, -104.9269

As the first permanent settlement of Colfax County, Rayado, which means "streaked" in Spanish, was an important hub along the Mountain Branch of the Santa Fe Trail. The townsite was in the extreme southeast corner of the famed Maxwell Land Grant owned by Lucien Maxwell, who also founded the town as a wagon train stop. Maxwell sold this land in the 1920s to Waite Phillips, an American oil man, who then donated 127,000 acres of his ranch in New Mexico to the Boy Scouts of America.

This land, an astounding 1.5 million acres, was first granted to Carlos Beaubien and his business partner, Guadalupe Miranda, by the Mexican government in 1841. After Lucien Maxwell married Beaubien's daughter, land was given to him as well; there, he built Rayado. Piñon and juniper forests dotted with ponderosa pines and cottonwoods and grassy plains at the foothills of the Sangre de Cristo (Blood of Christ) Mountains make a stunning setting for this ghost town.

During Maxwell's time, the plains of northern New Mexico were a hotbed for Native attacks, so they were not highly populated and travel there was extremely dangerous. In order to encourage more settlers to move into the region, Maxwell convinced frontiersman Christopher "Kit" Carson to move to Rayado in 1849 to give the impression that the town was in a safe area. A reproduction of Carson's home and frontier fort is now the Kit Carson House and Museum, where reenactments are held with the staff dressed in period clothing. A federal garrison of U.S. Army Dragoons were based in the town in 1850 until nearby Fort Union could be completed. The Kit Carson House and Museum is seven miles south of the Philmont Boy Scout Ranch on NM-21 as you return to Taos.

VAN HOUTEN

36.7923, -104.5658

Located near Dawson, the town of Van Houten is probably far less known than its neighbor. Starting life as a mining camp named Willow in 1902, its name was changed to reflect the Dutch president of the coal company. Ornately gated mine entrances, concrete foundations, mining equipment and dilapidated structures dot the landscape around the once-flourishing town, which is in a surprisingly good state of preservation. Many of the homes and buildings were constructed with poured concrete and hollow blocks to form carefully grided neighborhoods that housed the 1,500 residents who called Van Houten home.

It is also suggested that you visit the NRA Whittington Center, which is home to the Frank Brownell Museum of the Southwest, which features a large collection of vintage firearms, during your stay, as it includes a library and gift shop. You will be able to see the deep ruts that were carved into the landscape by the many wagons which traveled the famous Santa Fe Trail. Ornately gated mine shafts close off the stonework at the mouth of the mines, which are now being used for storage. The town of Van Houten is currently being preserved by its current owners.

6

UNION COUNTY

FOLSOM

36.84502, -103.91774

Comanche, Ute and Jicarilla Apache tribes roamed the region now known as Union County for the first half of the nineteenth century, but Native activity in the region dates to 9000 and 8000 BCE. It is from this culture that many artifacts have been unearthed in archaeological excavations—revealing the famous "Folsom Point," which gave evidence to man existing in the region since the Pleistocene Age over twenty thousand years ago.

At the junction of NM-325 and NM-456 in Union County sits the town of Folsom, named for the bride-elect of President Grover Cleveland, Frances Folsom, who explored the tiny village during her whistle stop tour. Folsom was so charming that the townsfolk decided to name their town after her when it gained its post office in 1888.

Folsom once had the largest stockyards west of Fort Worth and was called Ojo (meaning "eye"), Madison and Ragtown before it was finally named Folsom in 1888. It's hard to believe today, but Folsom once boasted a population of over one thousand before its decline in 1908, which was also the year a flood washed away most of the town and killed seventeen people. A monument in the Folsom Museum (which is one of the few businesses still open in the town) honors Sally J. Rooke, a dispatcher, who perished while manning her station to warn the townsfolk of the impending danger. Today, the town's population hovers around eighty.

Folsom Hotel has been a mercantile store, hotel and private residence in its history.

GRENVILLE

36.5928, -103.6163

Located between Des Moines and Clayton, New Mexico, on U.S.-64/87, Grenville is often forgotten but is well worth the effort to visit. Its ominous-looking wooden houses harken back to much earlier days and give you the true sense of what it must have been like to live on these open plains.

As a railroad town, Grenville was founded as a camp for the rail workers who were laying new track for the Denver and Fort Worth Railroad, which was absorbed by the Burlington Railroad. Platted in July 1888, several years after the camp was established and several months after the last spike of the railroad had been driven on March 14, 1888, Grenville became a supply and shipping hub for the ranches and farms that surrounded the town. Frijoles, or beans, were the primary crop raised on the plains of northeastern New Mexico, but it was the infamous Dust Bowl and end of the railroad that were the demise of Grenville.

Today, several of the town's buildings remain, including a restored Texaco station, stores, homes and a school building in a beautiful open plain setting. The Windsong Saloon and school/church are some of the most beautiful buildings in a ghost town setting in the state.

MADISON

36.8809, -103.87357

Having the distinction of being the first town established in Union County in 1864, Madison was named after its first settler, Madison Emery. A post office was established there in 1877, but Madison became an official ghost town in 1888, when the Colorado and Southern Railroad bypassed the town for nearby Folsom.

Being so close to the Oklahoma Territory in the 1860s, Madison was seen as a perfect hideout for outlaws running from the law. One such outlaw was Captain William Coe, who led a band of outlaws out of Kenton, Oklahoma. The bandits had a hideout known as "Robber's Roost" just north of Kenton, and when they got word that their haven was about to be raided, the gang headed to Madison, New Mexico. Coe was eventually captured in Madison by the U.S. Cavalry, with the help from Madison Emery's wife and son-in-law. Other gang members scattered to avoid capture and were never seen in the town of Madison again. An old gristmill foundation is almost all that remains of the former outlaw hideout. Many of Madison's residents moved to Folsom, leaving Madison to its ruin.

7

MORA COUNTY

LOMA PARDA

35.84671, -105.07584

A quiet farming community that was established in northern New Mexico in the 1830s would probably not have made the history books if not for the construction of nearby Fort Union. With the arrival of the soldiers, some community members seized the opportunity to cash in on the boredom of the troops by building saloons and dance halls for their enjoyment. These establishments attracted many shady characters to the tiny village in the form of outlaws, gamblers and prostitutes—as well as cowboys and teamsters from the Santa Fe Trail.

As you walk into this tiny village and cross the lazy Mora River, canopied with ancient cottonwoods, you would never know the amount of danger you would have been in in 1852, when the area's population had swollen to include over four hundred hardened souls. It was said Loma Parda was giving Tombstone and Dodge City, Kansas, a run for their money, wickedness-wise. Soldiers were murdered, robbed of their winnings and pay, as well as spending a good amount of time in the hospital due to venereal disease and alcohol poisoning. One enterprising gentleman ran a wagon service from Loma Parda to Fort Union at the cost of one dollar per round trip, which was still too expensive for the soldiers, so they would walk or ride their military mounts into town.

Julian Baca's Dance Hall was a headache for nearby Fort Union.

Much to the dismay of the town's permanent residents, Loma Parda, which means "gray hill," received the dubious moniker of "Sodom on the Mora" by an officer named Hollister. He felt the town had earned this name due to its wild and sinful reputation for violence and debauchery. One of the more famous stories of Loma Parda involves a highly inebriated cowboy, rumored murderer James Lafer, who scooped his lady of choice off the street, draped her over the cantle of his saddle and rode his horse into Julian Baca's twenty-four-hour saloon. As locals said, when the horse refused to drink the alcohol that was placed before him, the drunk pulled out his revolver and shot the poor animal, killing it. Not swayed by the commotion he caused, the cowboy, most likely intoxicated on the local favorite, Loma Lightning (said to be a particularly vicious whiskey), continued with his rabble-rousing without a care, leaving his horse dead on the saloon floor.

The activities that Loma Parda provided were too much of a temptation for the soldiers of Fort Union, who ended up going AWOL and leaving the fort, which was seven miles away, with little to no protection. Ladies of ill repute flocked to the small town and utilized not only the brothels there but also the small caves in the area for their activities. Street

Above: Earning the name "Sodom on the Mora" Loma Parda was open twenty-four hours a day.

Right: Outlaws, gamblers and prostitutes made of the majority of the population.

prostitutes from Santa Fe would trade their wares for stolen items from the fort. In six months, it was reported by the fort that the army had lost 9,379 pounds of bacon, 5,254 pounds of sugar and 4,303 pounds of coffee, as well as soap, candles and dried fruits. To deter the women from coming to the fort to tempt the men, Captain Sykes captured three of them, put them in the stockade in the middle of the fort and shaved their heads. From then on, the caves around the fort have been known as "Bald Woman's Caves." The captain soon found out that it wasn't the ladies' hair that attracted the men.

Loma Parda began to fade into history, as Fort Union became unnecessary. The post office was open until 1900, but the town was not mentioned in the census after 1910. Farming continued in the beautiful valley until World War II, but it was abandoned completely soon after the war, when the only bridge into town was washed away in a flood in 1948. A footbridge is the only access today. As you walk the town, know that shadowy figures have been reported previously by other visitors, which is not surprising, given Loma Parda's violent past.

Travel north on I-25 to Exit 364 at Watrous; then turn left at the junction of NM-446 and NM-161. Follow NM-161 for six miles northwest of Watrous, toward Fort Union. Pass the turnoff to the Rio Mora National Wildlife Refuge; continue and turn right at the next road (it will be unpaved and possibly a bit rough with gravel for eight miles). Park at the bridge over the Mora River and cross on foot. Please be respectful of the buildings and land, as they are privately owned. The old will be mixed in with the new in some areas and you will find two peaceful cemeteries further up the dirt road.

WATROUS

35.7906, -104.98167

Just east of I-25, near the historical site of Fort Union, sits a small, three-street village that was once known as La Junta de los Rios Mora y Sapello (meaning "the Juncture of the Mora and Sapello Rivers"). And since it was on the point of the Mountain Branch and Cimarron Cutoff of the Santa Fe Trail, it proved to be quite prosperous. Established in 1843 by John Scolly, who received a Mexican land grant, La Junta began as a farming community that provided fresh milk, cheese and produce to the travelers along the trail. Established in 1846, La Junta continued to grow,

Watrous was a trading hub on the Santa Fe Trail.

Samuel B. Watrous House features twenty rooms.

attracting Alexander Barclay, who built an outpost that came to be known as "Barclay's Fort" nearby.

The area was then settled by William B. Tipton and his brothers, Enoch and Samuel Watrous. After William Tipton married Mary Watrous, the twelve-year-old daughter of Samuel, a freighter partnership was formed between the two men. Samuel B. Watrous donated his land for the right-of-way of the railroad that was to be built through the town. He was said to have been surprised to see the name "Watrous" as the new station's name. Railroad officials told him it was the least they could do for such a "public-spirited citizen." In 1886, Samuel Watrous reportedly committed suicide after the suicide of his son, Samuel Jr. But this story was questioned then, and his death remains a mystery today.

Today, the tiny town is home to approximately 135 residents, who all live in and around the twenty-one original surviving structures. Most of the buildings in Watrous were constructed before 1870, and some of the thousands of trees that were planted by Samuel Watrous still exist. Be sure to stop into the historic Watrous Coffee House on your way to view the Watrous House (Watrous Valley Ranch) on NM-61; you will not be disappointed by the tasty pastries and delicious coffee drinks available there. The Watrous House is one of New Mexico's finest examples of territorial architecture and is listed in the National Register of Historic Places.

8

HARDING COUNTY

MILLS

36.08531, -104.25526

Established in 1888, Mills is in the Kiowa National Grasslands, near Roy, New Mexico, on NM-39. The town was named after Springer rancher and attorney Melvin W. Mills, who was also a legislator, district attorney, judge, and supporter of the infamous "Santa Fe Ring." Mills shipped the fruit from his fourteen thousand trees and the cattle that he raised by railroad to supply the famous Harvey Houses, which were springing up along the railways. Mills also had a few scrapes with the dangerous gunfighter Clay Allison, who was an opponent to the Santa Fe Ring in the Colfax County War and nearly dealt vigilante force on Mills for his alleged part in the murder of Reverend Tolby of Elizabethtown. When the Canadian River overflowed and flooded, Mills lost everything. In 1925, when Mills was dying, he asked to be taken to his beloved twenty-two room mansion in Springer (now being restored), which had been foreclosed on, to die on a cot in the drawing room of the three-story mansion. His request was honored.

The town has only a few remaining foundations and row houses left over from its heyday, but it provides a perfect glimpse into pioneer living on the plains. When the Santa Fe Railroad came through the area, Mills grew exponentially, to a reported population of three thousand by 1913. The town comprised a post office, dance hall, two saloons, a bank, a barbershop,

The Mills Mansion in Springer is a symbol of riches to rags.

Mills, New Mexico, was named for attorney Melvin Mills. *Courtesy of the Library of Congress.*

a hospital with four doctors, three stores, five hotels, three churches, a theater and a school. The post office was opened in 1898 but was closed by 1908; it has since reopened and is the only building still in operation in the town today (but only on Saturday).

Floods, drought, the Great Depression and the Dust Bowl all played huge roles in the demise of Mills. Farm Security Administration photographer Dorothea Lange would visit Mills in the final death throes of the town in 1935 to capture some of her most famous images of heartbreak.

Nearby Mills Canyon (also known as the Canadian River Canyon) provides for opportunities to camp and was used by outlaws of the past to escape the long arm of the law. This canyon is home to green meadows, red sandstone cliffs and rock formations along the winding Canadian River with a nine-hundred-foot-deep rift. The National Forest Service says to use caution when navigating Mills Canyon, as it has a narrow, steep and winding road, for which a high-centered vehicle is recommended.

9

SAN MIGUEL COUNTY

LA LIENDRE

35.4223, -105.0506

It is written that La Liendre can be loosely translated to "a sting of nits," or "mosquito," in English, and this sleepy village twenty miles southeast of Las Vegas, New Mexico, was plagued with the buzzing insects to the extreme. Stacked rock ruins are all that remain of the originally named "Los Valles de San Antonio," which was established around 1840. The post office was intermittently run from 1878 to 1880, 1882 to 1884 and, finally, from 1906 to 1942.

Picturesque canyon scenery surrounds La Liendre, painted with hues of yellow, green, red and brown. Piñon, junipers and cholla cactuses dot the countryside and lend a natural form of landscaping to the ruins left behind along the Gallinas River Valley.

When the town was at its peak, La Liendre sported a post office, church, adobe homes and, of course, a saloon. The ranching community is now no more than a few collapsing buildings and a lonesome cemetery. La Liendre is a true ghost town, with no residents, but you can visit the town by traveling south on NM-67 for approximately nine miles to a fork in the road. Take the right fork for 4.2 miles. It is vitally important to close all stock gates behind you on the way in and on the way out. Ranchers are tolerant people, but they do not take well to losing their livelihood due to negligence of others.

SAN GERONIMO

35.58004, -105.39529

With a history dating to 1835, San Geronimo has witnessed much of New Mexico's turbulent past. As with many of the other early settlements in the territory, residents were plagued with frequent attacks by the Native populations, so they would build their homes close together for protection.

In 1879, the Atchison, Topeka and Santa Fe Railroad began to lay track near the town. A contract was made with Eugenio Romero to supply the ties needed for the new track, which sparked the need for a sawmill. This industry supplied San Geronimo with employment, and the town began to grow.

The town's Catholic church was built in 1906 and a school the following year in 1907. A cemetery sits approximately a half a mile from the picturesque church, with the most recent burial being 1977. Many of the headstones read 1898. These poor souls may have been victims to the smallpox epidemic which was devastating the surrounding pueblos between 1898 and 1899.

TERERRO

35.74198, -105.67502

Copper was king in the Tererro Mine in 1882, but by the mid-1920s, miners were pulling silver, gold, lead and zinc from the hills surrounding the mining camp. The ore was then sent to nearby Glorieta for milling and concentration via an aerial tramway to the "El Molino" site on Alamitos Creek.

From 1916 to 1926, the town was owned by the Goodrich-Lockhart Company, which changed the name of the camp to the Pecos River Mining Company, and then the American Metal Company took over as its profits increased between 1926 and 1939. The town began to boom with the large amount of ore being extracted, attracting over three thousand souls to the area, with six-hundred of them working at the mine. As the town grew, so did the need for amenities, such as a school, a hospital, restaurants, a jail, boardinghouses and, of course, saloons. A flourishing red-light district known as "Chihuahua" also provided entertainment for the miners, who were mainly Hispanic.

A miners' strike in 1939 was the demise of the town, as the mines were left without workers. A contract between the State of New Mexico and the American Metal Company was made to restore the townsite to a wilderness area when it was vacated. Unfortunately, not much, if any, of the original townsite remains, but you can still visit the region, which is stunningly beautiful. In the 1990s, a mining company contaminated the river and caused the deaths of over ninety thousand fish. After $28 million was spent by the state, the mine was declared a superfund site, although most of the contaminates had been cleaned up and contained. Water tests in 2010 showed no instances of zinc or cadmium, and no more fish have died since 1991. A new mining operation has recently voiced a desire to explore in the area, which has met much ongoing opposition in the region.

Today, a modern general store exists as the last stop for necessities for campers or fishermen. If you are going fishing, please make sure you purchase a fishing license before putting a hook in the river. Also, be mindful that the closest restaurants are in Pecos and then Santa Fe. The Lisboa Springs Fish Hatchery is one of the oldest hatcheries in New Mexico; it raises about 135,000 rainbow trout each year, which are then released into the Pecos River. Monastery Lake is next to the hatchery and provides a gorgeous setting for the Pecos Benedictine Monastery, which is also known as Our Lady of Guadalupe Abbey. The monastery provides spiritual retreats and has an interesting gift shop. Originally owned in 1947 by Trappist monks from Rhode Island, the monastery was sold to Benedictine monks from Wisconsin in 1985.

Tererro is also known as one of the best spots in New Mexico to see three species of hummingbirds: the Broadtail, Rufus and Calliope. The birds arrive in March to spend their springs and summers in New Mexico before returning to the Caribbean. You can hear their distinct humming sounds as they buzz by your head on their way to the feeders found everywhere in Tererro.

Toward the end of NM-63, north of Pecos, New Mexico, is the edge of the Pecos Wilderness in the Santa Fe National Forest. Head north from Pecos for approximately fifteen miles on a winding mountain road, which is slow going. Please be mindful of the rocks on both the road and possibly falling from the mountains through which the road is cut. The trip to the area will take close to thirty minutes from Pecos.

Be warned, the Holy Ghost Campground at Tererro is touted by several online blog sites as the most haunted campground in New Mexico. Legend states a priest either killed people from the nearby pueblo of Pecos or was killed by the people of the pueblo, depending on which story you read. Either way, the spirit of the priest is said to still wander the forest, and other paranormal activity is widely reported.

TREMENTINA

35.46977, -104.52776

Roofless rock walls that date to the 1800s and hold the secrets of the past are scattered against a bluff overlooking Trementina Creek in San Miguel County. This town was named for the Trementina (Nementina) tribe, which may have been an early Lipan Apache group that roamed the Texas Panhandle and eastern New Mexico. Since the name means "turpentine" in Spanish, it is unknown how it was acquired by these Natives.

Families from Los Velles de San Agustin, Los Fuertes, Chaperito and La Aguila moved to Trementina, largely due to the sale of land on the Antonio Ortiz Grant. The townsite was established at the turn of the century by Santiago and Juana Blea and was promoted by a tenacious Presbyterian medical missionary and schoolteacher named Alice Blake, who originally came to La Aguila in 1887. Trementina survived, among other things, a diphtheria epidemic, water poisoning from wool washing and railroad tie pickling upstream, the Depression, drought and World War II.

Determined to convert the residents to be Presbyterians, Alice Blake needed to build a church. The Jaramillo family members were stonemasons and so skilled at their craft that they could build an entire home in just three days' time. A 150-seat church was erected and housed the school. Tragically, in 1916, the church burned, but since it was constructed of flagstone, it was largely reusable. By 1902, there were forty children enrolled in the school, where they learned English and maintained their native tongue, Spanish. A memorial bell was commissioned for the fine building, which the residents were so grateful for, they built a desk for Blake from the shipping crate.

Through her medical training, Blake taught the residents the importance of sanitation and hygiene. Also, due to the town's isolated location, the art of first aid and midwifery were also instilled. Trementina was hit with malaria, typhoid fever, tuberculosis and diphtheria. The latter was treated by antitoxins given by a Las Vegas doctor to fifty-six citizens, including Alice Blake, who survived. Unfortunately, many small children were not so lucky.

In 1916, Trementina received a large gift of fruit and shade trees, which were promptly eaten by a goat that was purchased to provide milk for a local baby. The town flourished as a sheep ranching community with a hospital, a larger school and a community house. By the start of the World War I in 1918, Alice Blake had left the community for a year, but she came back to retire with a pension in 1931. By the end of World War II, young soldiers, who had seen more than their small village, yearned for the nation's large cities and took their families away in search of more opportunities. Since the Korean War, Trementina has become an official ghost town.

Today, echoes of the past are mixed with remnants of rock dwellings and touches of the modern world, such as old glass-tank gas pumps. Strange cuts in the surrounding landscape have also been noticed and are said to have been a secret compound/landing zone for the Scientologists to guide their leader back to Earth. The compound is said to also contain tunnels, immense steel slabs and barracks—proof New Mexico is anything but mundane.

To get to Trementina, travel east from Las Vegas, New Mexico, on NM-104/65 for approximately fifty miles. You will be surrounded by red mesas and open landscapes, where the Comanche, Apache and bison once roamed.

10

GUADALUPE COUNTY

Cuervo

35.03117, -104.40859

Amid the many claims of paranormal experiences in Cuervo, New Mexico, by visitors and residents alike, none have been substantiated, but this small town certainly has a spooky feel. Highly accessible off I-40, 16.8 miles east of Santa Rosa, Cuervo, which means "crow" in Spanish, has attracted many to stop and explore—but some of these visitors are without good intentions.

Evidence of criminal activity is visible when you look in a few of the abandoned buildings; such evidence was discovered by author John Mulhouse as he explored the back room of the one of the best preserved buildings in Cuervo—the Catholic church, which sported dozens of pairs of women's underwear, tank tops and pornography nailed to the walls, with explicit handwritten notes on the wall by each item.

This disturbing evidence was reported to law enforcement, which initiated an investigation, and made the evening news in Albuquerque. The fear was that a serial rapist was utilizing the interstate to commit horrible crimes. After these items were discovered, they were taken down—presumably by law enforcement—but similar items reappeared in nearly the same configuration in a building seven miles to the west of Cuervo. These items were discovered by a couple of women who were photographing the old buildings. The back room is now boarded off, and the church is always locked.

Cuervo's church and parsonage have seen much evil.

Another revolting scene unfolded at the Baptist church just down the road from the Catholic church, which was used by Satanic cults during the 1970s and 1980s. These cults left symbols of evil graffitied on the walls, pointing toward devil worship and sexual activities. These scenes were graphic and highly explicit, a shocking occurrence inside a former church.

Originally a railroad town, Cuevo stayed alive with Route 66 literally running through the heart of the town, holding it together until I-40 replaced Route 66. At that time, many of the town's longtime residents were forced from their homes. The only way for Cuervo to survive the interstate was to have exit ramps built for access—the only problem was that these ramps cost upward of $1 million each, a cost the town could not absorb. Today, approximately fifty-eight brave souls still inhabit the town, which retained its zip code until 2011.

Clapboard, adobe and red-brick buildings and homes are striking sights against the red bluffs located behind the town, and they attract many photographers. but if any deserted town in New Mexico was haunted, it would be Cuervo. The feeling of a presence around you always is daunting.

Red-stone and adobe dwellings against the basalt mountains are typical New Mexico.

This feeling, mixed with the evil that occurred at the site, makes the aura of the town foreboding, to say the least. It's easy to say that the only comfortable inhabitants of these derelict ruins are the ever-present rattlesnakes.

I strongly advise for everyone to follow the advice of law enforcement and other authors who have written about Cuervo—this town should be taken off your list of visits. If you want to see this town, view the many videos online. Reports of visitors being followed and harassed are commonplace in the tiny village. The residents want their homes to be left alone, but with the news and social media attention they have experienced over recent years, this is becoming far more difficult. If you do decide to visit, please don't go alone for your own safety; tell someone where you are and always keep your cellphone charged and with you. A set of snake guards would also be an excellent idea, since large rattlesnakes have been reported to inhabit the buildings.

Pintada

34.88228, -105.07222

Pintada means "painted" in Spanish, and the town was most likely named for the colors in the arroyo nearby. Pintada Canyon was reported to have been settled in the early nineteenth century by a dozen families from Mexico. This settlement is on the north side of Cañon de Las Piedra Pintada (Canyon of the Painted Rock), and it sported a mercantile store, church, school and, as always, a saloon. Pintada was started as a ranching community and continues the tradition today. Pintada was also supported by a copper mine, which was located at an elevation of 5,059 feet.

The painted canyon contains many petroglyphs on its sandstone walls and ceilings that were created by the Puebloan people who lived in the pueblo ruins still found in the area (not to be confused with Pueblo Pintado near Chaco Canyon in northwestern New Mexico). Other tribes, such as the Kiowa, Apache and Comanches, also called this area home. This town is located eight miles south of U.S.-66 and twenty-four miles west of Santa Rosa, nestled in the piñon and juniper forested foothills.

11

QUAY COUNTY

Montoya

35.09978, -104.06386

A sign on the side of an adobe building in the town still advertises "cold beer," but there nothing left of the saloon where the beverage was once served. Yet another railroad town for the Southern Pacific Railroad, Montoya was established in 1902 but was a victim of the interstate system that overtook Route 66. The Richardson Store, built in 1908, is listed in the National Register of Historic Places. Unfortunately, it is mere ruins today, but it once provisioned the many railroad workers who lived in and around Montoya. Located along Route 66 on NM-219, just off I-40, Montoya has several buildings to explore, as well as a cemetery and the Saint Joan of Arc Church just two hundred yards off the road.

Richardson Store in Montoya was a busy spot in its day.

Buildings constructed of red stone from the surrounding mountains make for an interesting visual. Adobe was also widely used, often covered with plaster to protect the delicate mud bricks. Today, these walls are likely covered in sometimes vulgar graffiti. Snakes are also prevalent in this area.

Take Exit 311 when traveling east to Tucumcari. Cross I-40 and follow the Frontage Road to the ruins of the Richardson Store; the church will be accessible a little farther up the frontage road to the first dirt road to the right. You will literally be in the middle of the opposing lanes of I-40.

NARA VISA

35.6066, -103.1001

Situated on the Canadian River Break, Nara Visa began life as a railroad town for the Chicago, Rock Island and Pacific Railroad, which was built in 1901. The town gained its name from the nearby Nara Visa Creek, which was thought to have been an Americanized version of the name of a sheepherder who lived in the area, Narvaez. It is thought that the English-speaking setters pronounced his name "Narvis," and it got corrupted further to Nara Visa. On the Texas–New Mexico border, Nara Visa claimed to have 112 residents in the 2000 census.

Henry F. King was the first section foreman for the railroad and the first person to live in the town of Nara Visa. Since the train depot was the only structure in the town in 1901, King and his wife lived in a boxcar that became a boardinghouse of sorts for others who needed a place to stay. By 1902, a section house, a dugout school and post office could be found in the town.

The Nara Visa Bank came into existence when Sim and Fred McFarland moved to the tiny hamlet from La Veta, Colorado, in 1902 to work on their uncle's ranch. Instead, they set up a boxcar store, which included a safe, on the other side of the tracks from the original townsite. Customers began entrusting their money to the brothers, who also cashed their "checks," which were written in those days on brown paper sacks or scraps of paper. The McFarlands eventually sold their business to John and Anastacia Burns and moved to Logan, New Mexico, to establish the McFarland Brothers Bank in 1904. Nara Visa School, also known as the Nara Visa Community Center, was built in 1925 by Joseph Champ Berry and is now listed in the National Register of Historic Places.

12
DE BACA COUNTY

TAIBAN

34.44007, -104.00913

Founded in 1906 by six families from Portales, New Mexico, the town of Taiban (pronounced "tie-ban") sits close to the border of Texas on NM-84 in southcentral New Mexico. It has been home to settlers since the late 1870s and was named for the nearby creek. It was a bustling town, even during Prohibition, when it was called the "bootlegging capital of eastern New Mexico." Most of the nearby Texas towns—a short hop over the state line—are in dry counties, where alcohol is not allowed.

Much to the dismay of the town's parishioners, many illegal transactions of alcohol took place in front of the now-most photographed church in eastern New Mexico. The clapboard church is the highlight of the town, cutting a scene of isolation against the wide-open sky and surrounding sand dunes. Looking like a Hollywood set straight out of a Clint Eastwood western, the Presbyterian church was most likely beautiful in its heyday, but today, it has fallen victim to vandals, graffiti artists and transients.

Billy the Kid has ties to Taiban, as this is where he and two of his friends were captured by Sheriff Pat Garrett in December 1880. It was once home to a bank, hotel, general store, school and cemetery. The only building operating there today is the post office. The Taiban Presbyterian Church and the Pink Pony Bar and Dancehall were constantly at odds. The church

Once a part of a thriving community, the Taiban Church now attracts photographers and the curious.

wanted the town to be dry, and others were more inclined to favor the Pink Pony. Of the two establishments, the church is the only one left standing.

As it did in other towns, the Great Depression took its toll on Taiban in 1933, when passenger service was discontinued to the town. Afterward, the town of four hundred residents died. At its peak, there were over 1,300 trains passing through the plains, each bringing potential residents with them. And then there were none.

YESO

34.43924, -104.60998

A modern post office, water tank and rock ruins are almost all that remain of Yeso (also known as "Yesso"), between Vaughn and Fort Sumner, New Mexico. As the end of the rail line, Yeso was founded in 1906 along Yeso Creek. The name Yeso translates to "chalk" or "gypsum," which explains the fact the water from Yeso Creek was undrinkable due to the high gypsum content, but luckily, the underground water source proved to be better.

A railroad town for the Atchison, Topeka and Santa Fe (ATSF) Railroad along the Belen Cutoff, Yeso played its part in central New Mexico in preventing the trains from having to navigate the steep grades of the Colorado Mountains. Yeso was also home to one of the first frame train depots to be built along the Belen Cutoff in 1906.

The railroad played a large part in the rise and fall of Yeso. *Courtesy of the Library of Congress.*

Yeso was dealt several hard blows along its way; although several ranchers and farmers attempted to make a go of the land surrounding the town, a severe drought sealed the deal, and families began to filter away. The invention of the diesel locomotive after World War II meant that trains no longer needed to stop in the town for water. When the steam locomotives were phased out completely, the town of Yeso also dwindled to four families.

A school, which was built in 1940 by the Works Progress Administration (WPA), is one of the only remaining buildings left in town, along with the remains of the Hotel Mesa, which was turned into a museum later, and a post office, which closed its doors in 1968. Yeso is described as a poor town; this was exemplified by a family of fifteen who lived in a tiny adobe home. During good weather, the boys of the family would sleep out under the stars. Beans and tortillas were typical everyday fare, and if anyone had meat, they would share with their neighbors.

PART III

NORTHWEST NEW MEXICO

13

RIO ARRIBA COUNTY

HOPEWELL

36.4352, -106.7825

Established in the late 1800s as a stream placer gold mining camp, Hopewell grew fast to boast a population of over two thousand, with a post office in operation from 1894 to 1906. It is thought the town got its name from Willard S. Hopewell, who had a cattle ranch and mining operations in the area around 1878. The townsite is located along the appropriately named Placer Creek, 9,500 feet high in the Tusas Mountains, and was said to have provided a good living for the residents until the gold ran out. Gold valued at more than $175,000 was removed during the mine's first three years of operation, with a grand total of $300,000 of production by 1910.

Today, Hopewell Lake, a man-made day-use lake, is located near the old townsite and provides some of the best trout fishing in the state, as well as hiking and camping opportunities for those interested. The group picnic shelter is built on the townsite, and the hiking trails in Carson National Forest are part of the Continental Divide Trail, which runs from Canada to Mexico. There are surviving prospect pits in the area, but there are also warnings about gold panning and removal. The Rocky Mountain Snowpack Program was established in Hopewell in 1993 to provide a network of snowpack sampling sites in the Rocky Mountain region from New Mexico to Montana.

The town is located twenty miles southeast of Chama between Tierra Amarilla and Tres Piedras, New Mexico, off NM-64.

SUBLETTE

36.9889, -106.23003

A railroad town built in 1880, Sublette sits high in the San Juan Mountains at an elevation of 9,281 feet. Starting life as a construction camp for the Denver and Rio Grande Railroad's narrow-gauge San Juan Branch, Sublette provided living quarters for crew members. When the town was constructed, it included a coal bunker, a speeder shed, a water tower and a couple of bunkhouses for the crew, as well as a home for the foreman and his family.

The Denver and Rio Grande Railroad ran on these tracks until 1967, when it became the rails for the Cumbres and Toltec Scenic Railroad, which

Sublette is now a stop on the famous Cumbres & Toltec Scenic Railway.

still runs sixty-four miles from Chama, New Mexico, to Antonito, Colorado, each summer at a whopping twelve miles per hour. If you have a chance to ride this historic route, please do so—you will not regret it. The stunning mountain scenery of tunnels, trestles and meadows will leave you breathless. You will be able to visit Sublette during your journey, as the train stops there to take water from the underground cistern (the water tower was dismantled in 1937). Thanks to the Friends of the Cumbres and Toltec for their efforts of historic preservation as they maintain the remaining buildings in Sublette for future generations to enjoy.

14

MCKINLEY COUNTY

Allison

35.52419, -108.78509

Once encompassing the entire valley, the Allison Mine was a large operation. Coal mining operations in the town were first started by Gus Mulholland and, later, Andrew Casna (who was killed during one of the many Native raids in the region, and his wife went back to Germany). Since she was not there to file the claim, it was purchased by Fletcher J. Allison in 1897, and the town of Allison was born.

By 1917, the property on which the town sat was sold to the Diamond Coal Company, making Allison a company-owned town. Company housing was modest, comprising a three- to four-room house furnished with the necessities of electricity and water. The coal company was also concerned about the health of its employees, so it set up tennis courts and organized a baseball team.

Serving as a suburb for Gallup, New Mexico (which was called Carbon City at that time), only 2.8 miles to the west, Allison reportedly has over five hundred residents, but they are mainly rural dwellers. The Atchison, Topeka and Santa Fe Railroad established a station between Allison and Twin Buttes, New Mexico, that was named West Yard and served as the coal shipping point for the mines.

GAMERCO

35.57224, -108.76536

As it was in the other towns surrounding Gallup, in Gamerco, coal mining was a way of life. Gamerco was founded in 1920, when the Gallup American Coal Company began sinking shafts into the massive coal deposits in the area. Before long, Gamerco supported over five hundred miners and their families. The name Gamerco is a consolidation of "Gallup American Coal Company." The mines, unfortunately, shut down in the 1960s, leaving a smokestack that towers over the remaining ruins of the once-busy town. Today, a few residents call Gamerco home, and you can find the smokestack and remains of the power plant in the town.

The coal company was extra vigilant when it came to the safety of its workers due to the disasters that saw so much loss of life in Dawson, New Mexico. Ninety percent of the underground miners in Gamerco were rescue and first aid certified and wore electric lamps. Only the use of low-heat explosives was allowed. Compared to today's miners' wages, Gamerco's miners' wages seem extremely low, at $5.60 for a seven-hour day—especially since no overtime was allowed. The men were in a continuous cycle of pay and owing the company store for necessities. Strikes were frequent for these reasons, and unions were highly discouraged. In 1933, the state militia was called in to break up a strike organized by the National Miners Union over low wages.

Gamerco closed for good in the 1960s, but some of remnants of its glory days remain, including the smokestack from the power plant. Located on an ominously named highway—the "Devil's Highway" or "Beast of a Highway" due to its numeration of 666—the area was said to be haunted or cursed by the Natives who lived there. The highway ran from Gallup, New Mexico, to Cortez, Colorado, but on January 1, 2003, the route number was changed to a less demonic number—U.S.-491. Gamerco is located three miles north of I-40, Exit 20 at Gallup.

15

SANDOVAL COUNTY

CABEZON

35.62642, -107.09782

Started in the 1870s as a farm and ranch community on the surrounding grazing land, Cabezon is one of the few settlements that was not connected to the mining industry. Cabezon also became an important stage stop between Santa Fe and Fort Wingate on the Prescott, Arizona route. Gaining its name from the nearby volcanic peak of the same name in 1891, Cabezon was one of the original towns on the then-raging Rio Puerco and is located approximately six miles from the village of San Ysidro on NM-44.

Since Cabezon is located on private land, trespassing is strictly prohibited. It is still visible from the road and includes an entire town, complete with a saloon, a blacksmith shop, a school, a church and a graveyard, all with the magnificent volcanic neck Cabezon Peak standing proudly at an eight-thousand-foot elevation in the background. The town was basically owned by a businessman named Richard Heller, who owned an eleven-room mansion in the town and was responsible for its constant growth. After Heller's death, the town began to dwindle, as he was one of the largest sources of income for Cabezon.

Sadly, in 1947, the Rio Puerco, which means "river of pigs" in Spanish (but the translation has been Americanized to mean "muddy river"), dried up after a series of devastating floods in 1880 and 1929. This contributed to

Above: Cabezon (which means "Big Head") Peak has been used as a landmark for centuries.

Right: San Jose De Cabezon Church has been restored and refurbished.

silt buildup as well and carved deep canyons from the sandy soil. Now, the river only flows during the monsoons.

Much has been written about Cabezon being haunted, with apparitions of cowboys, soldiers, orbs and strange mists being reported. The Navajo also tell tales about Cabezon (which means "head," as it is the head of a giant who was cut down by gods, causing his blood to congeal and form the El Malpais, "bad land"), and this area holds religious significance for the Navajo Nation and Pueblo people.

Hagan/Coyote

35.3172622, -106.313913

In 1904, the New Mexico Fuel and Iron Company came to the area northeast of Albuquerque to develop the coal deposits in the region, which were discovered in 1902. The town of Hagan was a planned community and was expected to have five hundred residents. It was named after railroad man William Hagan but was developed by Dr. Jean Justin DePraslin of New Orleans, Louisiana, in 1919 after the mines closed in 1910. Known as a gentleman entrepreneur, DePraslin was able to obtain $450,000 from multiple investors to establish the Hagan Coal Mine, which included miner housing, a power plant and other mining buildings, with a little to spare for a railroad spur, which was completed in 1924.

As with many other towns, the railroad was responsible for the prosperity in Hagan. A hotel, a school, a post office, restaurants and pool halls sprang up and did booming business until the coal ran out in 1930, causing a collapse of Hagan's economy. By 1933, the railroad was dismantled, and the entire town was abandoned before the start of World War II. Skeletons of buildings are all that remain to tell the story of this once-thriving town.

Three miles away from Hagan is the town of Coyote, which was also a coal mining community. But being bypassed by the railroad was Coyote's demise. It is important to note that both towns are on private property as part of the Diamond Tail Ranch, east of San Felipe Pueblo, and there are "no trespassing" and "keep out" signs everywhere—trespassing is strictly prohibited. Please heed these warnings—you will be able to see the ruins of both towns from the dirt road you take from behind the San Felipe Casino. Proceed about eight miles to Coyote, which will be on the left just before the road disappears into an arroyo. Watch for adobe ruins that blend in well with the surrounding countryside. Hagan will be on a bluff about three miles past the arroyo. Caution: do not attempt to drive on this road after it has rained. You will get stuck in the mud, and sometimes, the road has been known to be closed.

LA VENTANA

35.8272446, -106.9717067

La Ventana came to be in the late 1870s, when Hispanic people began to settle the land around the Rio Puerco. The only problem was this was also the land the Navajo tribe called home, and they were not pleased with their new neighbors. Their constant raids and attacks forced the settlers to abandon La Ventana until 1914, when coal was discovered.

While a good supply of coal was being produced in the town between 1920 and 1930, factors such as the Great Depression and the Dust Bowl brought an end to the mining at La Ventana, and the town was abandoned once again. Today, the town consists of a few original structures and deserted buildings. Close to this region is the La Ventana Natural Arch, a beautiful element-carved sandstone arch in the El Malpais National Conservation Area. It is well worth a side trip to experience this stunning sculpture of Mother Nature.

CIBOLA COUNTY

BUDVILLE

35.07004, -107.52588

This quiet, unassuming hamlet on Route 66, near the Laguna Pueblo, gives off the aura of once being an All-American town, but its history is full of murder and mayhem. Howard Neal "Bud" Rice and his wife, Flossie, decided, with the construction of Route 66 in 1928, this location would be a gold mine for anyone who could cater to the needs of the throngs of travelers heading west. Soon, a gas station, a trading post and automotive repair buildings appeared there and were quickly dubbed "Budville."

As the only automotive repair and wrecking service between Albuquerque and Gallup, Budville was able to set its own prices. Bud also served as the justice of the peace and was notorious for issuing steep fines to outsiders for traffic or law violations.

In November 1967, tragedy struck when the store was robbed with four people inside. Bud; Flossie; Blanche Brown, an eighty-two-year-old retired schoolteacher who worked at the store part time; and a housekeeper, Nettie Buckley, faced the robbers, and when shots were fired, Blanche and Bud were killed. This incident earned the building the moniker "Bloodville." Although arrests were made, no one was convicted of this horrible crime.

Flossie continued to run the business and went on to marry a man named Max Atkinson. Six years later, Atkinson was killed in a fight only feet from

Budville Trading Post is the site of two unsolved murders.

where Bud had passed. Flossie then married for a third time, and this time, her husband passed away from natural causes in 1994. Through it all, Flossie kept the doors of the business open, but it eventually closed after sixty-six years of business.

McCarty's

35.06333, -107.68361

The Atchison, Topeka and Santa Railroad built a station called McCarty's in the 1880s, but the town was originally known as Santa Maria (this predated the railroad). McCarty was the name of a contractor who lived in the area when the railway was being built, so the company Americanized the name with the station.

McCarty's was not located on the original Route 66 and was basically a service station on the highway whenever the mother road was built. McCarty's has ancient roots, as this village was once used by the Acoma Pueblo tribe as a summer home, and before that, Native tribes had been in the region for more than ten thousand years. It was also occupied by the first

McCarty's was a railway station for the Atchison Topeka and Santa Fe Railroad. *Courtesy of the Library of Congress.*

Spanish explorers, including Francisco Vasquez de Coronado in the 1600s, until the Pueblo Revolt of 1680, when the Spanish were driven out of the area, not to return for twelve years. The Santa Maria Mission is a survivor of the Pueblo Revolt and sits proudly on the side of a hill off I-40.

One of the youngest lava flows in the state is the McCarty's Lava Flow, and it features an unusual occurrence of fire and ice known as the Bandera Volcano and Ice Cave—this is worth a side trip. Don't miss taking a tour of the nearby Acoma Pueblo (Sky City), as this is an awe-inspiring location as well.

Sawyer

35.1792, -108.2484

The beautiful Zuni Mountains in Cibola County are home to the logging communities of Sawyer, Diener and Copperton. Sawyer was the site of a sawmill that operated in support of the Zuni Mountain Railroad at the headwaters of Bluewater Creek when the town was established in the early 1900s. Although there were only thirty families living in the area, the town was able to support a saloon, a two-room schoolhouse, a village constable and a mercantile store.

To meet the demands of the railroad and surrounding towns, the three logging communities continuously worked to deforest the mountains. Albuquerque Lumber Company was one of Sawyer's largest clients for logs. Unfortunately, over-foresting was the demise of Sawyer; by 1919, the logs had run out, and the sawmills were closed. All that remains of the once-bustling mountain community are a few log structures in a beautiful, peaceful mountain setting.

The town is located on old forestry roads, which are not in great condition sometimes. Sawyer can be a bit of a challenge to visit, but it is obtainable in a two-wheel drive vehicle.

PART IV

SOUTHWEST NEW MEXICO

17

CATRON COUNTY

ALMA

33.2246, -108.5412

Starting life as Mogollon, the town eventually became known as Alma. In 1878, Captain Birney purchased the town and renamed it for his mother. Possibly due to the remoteness of Alma's location, the town was rumored to have attracted the attention of outlaws, including Butch Cassidy and Tom "Black Jack" Ketchum, and it had ties to Billy the Kid, as his stepfather, William Antrim, was a resident. The rugged countryside of the western New Mexico Territory was inspiration for Danish-American western artist Olaf Wieghorst, who worked on the Cunningham Ranch near Alma. Wieghorst's paintings and sketches often feature scenes from his time in the western states.

Butch Cassidy, the Sundance Kid and the Wild Bunch settled in Alma for a short time while working on the WS Ranch as cowboys. The ranch owner reported he was pleased with their work, as the incidences of cattle rustling stopped while they worked there. Pinkerton detective Charlie Siringo, who tracked and infiltrated the Wild Bunch, stated Butch Cassidy ran a saloon in Alma under the name of Jim Lowe.

Sergeant James C. Cooney originally laid out the town after his retirement from the army in 1876. Cooney had discovered large deposits of silver and gold in the region while he was on a scouting mission for the Eighth U.S. Cavalry from nearby Fort Bayard. The town was never fully developed with Cooney at the helm, as he was far more interested in the metals being pulled from the Mogollon Mountains and in staying alive after enduring numerous attacks by the Chiricahua Apache.

On April 28, 1880, during the Apache Wars, the Chiricahua Apache, led by the famed warrior Victorio, imparted a bloody raid on the towns of Cooney and Alma. Cooney was hit first, as three men were killed in the mining camp. Three other men, including James Cooney, were able to escape, but their pursuers eventually caught and killed them. The town's next attack was known as the Alma Massacre, in which a total of thirty-five people were killed. Many of the victims were sheepherders and their families. It was only when the troops from Fort Bayard arrived that the killers left the area. James Cooney was buried in a rock tomb next to his home that his brother and friends dynamited out from a huge boulder. This tomb is still considered a local attraction.

The town of Alma still exists, although it is mainly just a few remnants of adobe buildings, as well as a store, a restaurant, a few homes and a cemetery. Alma ranchers are in a different battle today, as the Mexican gray wolf was released on their ranchlands in 1998, creating a new type of danger for their livelihoods. This reintroduction program has been a source of conflict between ranchers, environmentalists and law enforcement alike, and it is a hotly debated issue in the state.

Near the Arizona border on U.S.-180, Alma has been pronounced a ghost town by the New Mexico Tourism Department, and it is situated in the breathtakingly beautiful Blue Range Wilderness in the Gila (HE-la) National Forest and Apache-Sitgreaves National Forest in Arizona, with stunning views of the Mogollon Mountains.

FRISCO

33.2372865, -108.8817289

San Francisco's name was shortened to Frisco and was a quiet ranching town four miles south of Reserve, New Mexico on the Tularosa River, which is known for flash flooding. Frisco was the scene of a famous gunfight between Elfego Baca, a well-known gunman/lawman, and reportedly eighty Texas cowboys.

On October 29, 1884, a local deputy (the legal part of this deputization is a bit sketchy), Elfego Baca, was asked by a local saloonkeeper to restrain a cowboy by the name of Charlie McCarty (or McCarthy, depending on the source), who had had too much to drink and was shooting up the place. Once he was able to disarm the cowboy, Baca arrested him and went to the local magistrate, who refused to hear the case, since McCarty worked for the powerful Slaughter Ranch. After hearing this, Baca decided to place the man under house arrest in the home of Geronimo Armijo.

McCarty's boss, Young Parham, and a mob of ranch hands showed up at Baca's door, demanding the release of their man. Baca refused, telling the men to move on or he would start shooting; they refused, and he did as he had threatened. During the fracas, Parham's horse reared and fell on him, crushing him to death. This ended the fight for a time. McCarty was tired the next day and received a five dollar fine for his merriment. Baca refused to return McCarty's weapon to him, taking it with him to his home. This action incited the cowboys to rally together to avenge the death of their boss and the arrest of McCarty.

The men surrounded the dwelling Baca was held up in and began to shoot, filling the adobe and wood structure with lead. Baca returned fire, resulting in the deaths of at least one of the men (Baca would report that he had killed four men and wounded eight). The gunfight lasted all day and well into the night for a reported thirty hours, which made many contemplate how Baca could survive such a violent attack by so many. Unknown to anyone, especially the cowboys, the floor of the hut where Baca had taken refuge sat approximately a foot and a half below its foundation level. Even after many attempts were made to flush Baca out of his position, including setting fire to the roof, which caused part of the roof to collapse in, Baca was found the next morning, cooking tortillas on the stove in the hut. This incident would be forever referred to as the "Frisco War," as the dwelling had a reported four hundred bullet holes afterward.

Law enforcement told Baca he would have to surrender himself to the courthouse in Socorro; Baca agreed, but only when guaranteed safe passage. Along the way, Baca was harassed by cowboys and survived at least two ambush attempts. Baca was found innocent on the charge of murder, as the door from Armijo's hut was entered into evidence, and he later became the sheriff of Socorro County. Baca practiced law in New Mexico from 1894 until his death on August 27, 1945, at the age of eighty. A movie titled *The Nine Lives of Elfego Baca* was filmed in Cerrillos, New Mexico, in 1957.

Baca was famous for his tactics of bringing outlaws to justice in New Mexico. His most famous method was to write the outlaw a letter, stating, "I have a warrant for your arrest. Please come in by ___ and give yourself up. If you don't, I'll know you intend to resist arrest, I will feel justified in shooting you on sight when I come after you." Baca was quoted in an interview as saying, "I never wanted to kill anybody, but if a man had it in his mind to kill me, I made it my business to get him first.'"

Mogollon

33.39673, -108.79423

An extremely narrow, hairpin winding road with limited visibility will take you into one of the best-preserved ghost towns in New Mexico. Please be aware of the open range and the possibility of livestock being on the road. If your stomach is settled enough as you approach the town, take notice of the narrow-gauge railroad tracks on the right-hand side of the road. These tracks served the Silver City, Piños Altos and Mogollon Railroad, which hauled the large amounts of ore pulled from the Mogollon Mountain Range behind the town. What are thought to be

Mogollon has a rich mining past and is said to be haunted. *Courtesy of the Library of Congress.*

Tailings from the Little Fannie Mine, which operated from the 1890s to 1952. *Courtesy of the Library of Congress.*

Dublin caves—small shelters blasted from the hillside for miners to live in temporarily—are temptations for exploration as well, but sadly, they are bolted shut.

How does one pronounce the name *Mogollon*, you ask? Officially, it is "moh-goh-yohn" with all long Os, but the locals are known to say "muggy-yohn." Named after a Spanish governor of New Mexico, Don Juan Ignacio Flores Mogollon, the town was established in 1876 and soon became one of the roughest mining towns in the territory. With a population of more than six thousand souls—mostly miners who worked in the "Little Fannie Mine"—you can imagine what living in this town was like.

Seventy-five miles from Silver City, New Mexico, Mogollon is home to almost one hundred historic buildings, which garnered a spot in the National Register of Historic Places for the town in 1987. The J.P. Holland General Store building now serves as the Silver Creek Hotel and can be rented for the night in most cases without a reservation, but you should call ahead just in case. During the town's heyday, there were five saloons, two extremely busy red-light districts, two hotels and a stage line there. According to legend,

There were between three thousand and six thousand miners in Mogollon in the 1890s.
Courtesy of the Library of Congress.

the Silver Creek Stage Line was robbed twenty-three times between 1872 and 1873 by the same person. Its treacherous seventy-five-mile-long daily journey from Mogollon to Silver City took a bone-jarring fifteen hours (this same journey will take a little over an hour by automobile today).

Due to many factors, the town's population began to diminish. The Mogollon Theater has a sign stating it was built in 1915, which is the same time telephone, water and electrical services came to the town. A saloon and general store next to the theater are not original to the town but were built in 1973 as a movie set for *My Name Is Nobody*. Many of the hazards faced by the residents of Mogollon included fire, flood and Apache raids, all of which threatened to destroy the town at any moment. Floods plagued the town, as it was built along Silver Creek, which produced five large flooding events. The area's most recent flooding event occurred in 2013 and stranded the residents and many tourists. Flood control and water diversion has since been implemented.

The Little Fanny Mine has astounding statistics from its short period of operation. Approximately $1.5 million worth of gold and silver were mined there in 1913 alone; this represented 40 percent of New Mexico's total precious metal yield. Silver proved to be the largest producer, coming in at two-thirds of the $20 million of gold and silver mined—a total of 18 million ounces of silver was produced. The Little Fanny Mine was a survivor while other mines were closing in the region, lasting until 1952.

Today, Mogollon is one of the best-preserved ghost towns in New Mexico and provides both history buffs and tourists a great sense of bygone days. Located seventy-five miles northwest of Silver City, New Mexico, off U.S.-180 at the end of NM-59, Mogollon sit at an elevation of 6,500 feet in the rugged Mogollon Range in the Gila Wilderness.

18

SOCORRO COUNTY

CLAUNCH

34.023248, -106.016997

This small town in central New Mexico that is known for growing pinto beans has had three names over the years. First, in 1890, the hamlet was known as DuBois Flats, and then it was known as Fairview around 1900. As the town had grown by 1930, it warranted a post office, but the name DuBois Flats was already taken, so town officials asked local cattle rancher L.H. Claunch if he would lend his name to the town. Claunch was agreeable, with one clause—a saloon would not carry his name. So, a saloon was never opened in Claunch.

Before 1930, the town was quite successful with its crop, and it had a processing plant to ready the beans for shipment. When the Great Depression, a terrible drought and the Dust Bowl hit, the triple whammy reduced Claunch to a few hardy residents. As was the custom, the Works Progress Administration (WPA) came in and built a school, but it would close by the 1950s. Only a few families remained on the windswept plains in the 1960s and 1970s to live among the pronghorn antelope.

Through it all, their faith was strong. In 1916, the Torrance County Singing Convention was formed as a formal gathering, where religious hymns would be sung in an arbor. This convention, which began on the fourth Sunday of April, with others in June, August and October, attracted not only local

Left: Claunch School has been tested by the hands of time.

Below: Rusty gold in a Claunch field, which once grew pinto beans.

people but those from other states as well. Hours and hours of singing was followed by massive amounts of food provided by the participants. It is said these conventions still happen but on a much smaller scale.

In the name of progress, a test of the atomic bomb was detonated in 1945 approximately forty miles from Claunch. The fallout from this test was devastating to several communities. Reports of cows turning white from the radiation were prevalent—so much so that ranchers would take their curious cows to the regional fairs to show them off. Sadly, the quaint little town of religious singers and pinto bean growers had become part of the "Downwinders' Society," with their land, plants, water and animals contaminated by the ten pounds of plutonium that joined with the soil (plutonium has a half-life of twenty-four thousand years). The blast went seven miles past the atmosphere, and the ash fell for days following the detonation. Residents in the affected areas were not warned of this action, and as of today, New Mexico downwinders have not been compensated for their miseries, and cancer rates remain extremely high in the blast area.

KELLY

34.08312, -107.20531

Kelly is considered a true ghost town since it has no residents. The town once boasted a population of nearly three thousand. When you arrive at the settlement, the first thing you will notice is the 121-foot-tall headframe looming over the massive tailing piles. The mining equipment that is scattered around was used in the mining operation that was started in the 1860s, when J.S. Hutchason found an outcropping of lead ore in the surrounding mountains. "Old Hutch," as he was called, founded the Juanita and Graphic Mines, with Patrick H. Kelley staking a claim he named after himself. When the claim was filed at the Socorro County Courthouse, an error was made—the last "e" was removed from the Kelley name. The town has gone by Kelly ever since.

The Kelly Mine headframe was erected by Gustav Billing and was constructed from a kit from Carnegie Steel Works of Passaic, New Jersey. This kit was designed by famed architect Alexander G. Eiffel, who designed the Eiffel Tower in Paris, France. When the ore ran out, the miners slowly moved to nearby Magdalena, leaving this beautiful relic of mining history behind to weather the elements on its own.

Carnegie Steel Works mine headframe stands at 121 feet tall.

Silver, lead and silver were pulled from the hills surrounding Kelly.

The road to Kelly is paved from Magdalena until you reach the San Jose Church; from then on, it is an extremely rocky road. A four-wheel drive vehicle is strongly advised for traveling to the town. Otherwise, you should park at the church and walk the short distance to the main headframe—good hiking boots are suggested here as well.

RILEY

34.38062, -107.22976

Starting life as Santa Rita, the community of Riley was formed in 1883 by fourteen Mexican American homesteader families who moved there from the Lemitar and San Acacia area, and it was founded by Pedro Aragon. With a good supply of water in the Rio Grande Valley, Riley was a farming or ranching community. Santa Rita's name was changed to Riley after a local sheepherder in 1890 when the town was granted a post office (the name Santa Rita was already being used by a town in Grants County, near Silver City).

Known as both Riley and Santa Rita, this town has an identity crisis.

In the late 1890s, a mine shaft was dug northwest of the town in a speculative search for gold or silver. It has since been discovered that this was a part of a popular mine speculator scam running during this era. Socorro was known to have vast supplies of silver, which was mined mainly by the Native people in the region, so investors were easy to fool with in the hopes of great riches. Deposits of coal and manganese were found in 1897, and the town's population grew to 150. When the mines closed, the post office closed, and when the water table dropped in 1931, the town of Riley's fate was sealed.

After a devastating flood in 1952, the irrigation ditches were washed away, making farming difficult once again. Many of the town's residents decided to move to Magdalena, Socorro or Pie Town. Today, the town is abandoned, with a few remnants of better times still visible. The Santa Rita Church is lovingly maintained by the members of the old community and on May 22, the feast of Santa Rita, a special mass is given by the local priest, with a picnic for the attendees held afterward.

Riley is located twenty miles north of Magdalena on Cibola National Forest Road 354. The first part of the journey is accessible by two-wheel-drive vehicles, but with heavy rains and flooding in the area over the years, the road tends to change and is maintained by the U.S. Army Corps of Engineers. Once you cross the Rio Salada, you will see a dilapidated building on your left, and farther up the road, which you could walk, if necessary, you will come across an old school building, a church and a cemetery—although they may be hidden from view. A line of dilapidated adobe cabins can be found if you head in an eastern direction from the church (a four-wheel-drive vehicle is recommended for this route). Do not attempt this trip during the monsoon season, as flash floods are likely to occur and are extremely dangerous.

19

SIERRA COUNTY

CHLORIDE

33.33868, -107.67781

If you could only visit one ghost town in Sierra County, I would highly recommend visiting Chloride. After exiting I-25, you will travel on a narrow two-lane highway with no shoulder. Please use caution, as there will be livestock on the road along with many dips and sharp hairpin turns on the way. This scenic—yet occasionally perilous—drive will lead you to one of the best-preserved ghost towns in New Mexico.

The first sight you will see is a sign that says you have entered the Chloride National Forest (ironically, the forest has only one tree). This tree, which is showing its age under the ravages of harsh weather, is also referred to as the "hanging tree." As ominous as this may sound, you may rest assured that no one was ever hanged from this tree. Chloride basically grew from thirteen residents to three thousand after word about the silver deposit discovery of Englishman Harry Pye, known as the "Pye Lode," spread. As a result of this discovery, nine saloons popped up in the town, so when one—or more—of the patrons got a bit too rowdy, they were taken to the tree, dunked in the horse trough underneath it and chained to it until they could behave.

In 1923, the owners of the mercantile store boarded up their windows and moved away. When Don Edmund and his wife, Dona, purchased the town in 1976, the store was reopened. What they found inside was a time

Above: Chloride had over twenty-seven buildings but no church.

Left: "The Hanging Tree" on Wall Street also marks the center of town.

Left: The owner of Chloride, Don Edmund, is also the museum curator and tour guide.

Below: Pioneer Store is now the fascinating Chloride Museum.

capsule, as the items were intact (except for the foodstuffs) and still on the shelves; they were just covered in massive amounts of bat guano and rat droppings. Once this was cleaned out and everything was sterilized, every item was returned to its exact spot, and the Pioneer Store Museum was opened to the public. During my time in Chloride, I was honored with a private tour of the museum by Don Edmund, who is a delightful host as the heart and soul of Chloride. He is extremely knowledgeable and loves to speak about his beloved town, which he and his wife restored. The residents of Chloride are also delightful and made me feel right at home.

Chloride's male population grew rapidly, leading the city council to offer a free lot of land to the first woman who moved to Chloride. There are no records about who this lucky woman was, but she got a great deal. The population soon rose to three thousand, with seven saloons popping up in the town. One of those saloons, the Monte Cristo, now serves as an art gallery that features artwork from artists in the area.

Cuchillo

33.23591, -107.36059

As a stage stop on the Armstrong Brothers of Chloride Stage Line, Cuchillo served as a welcome opportunity to rest for travelers and horses alike. The town's flagstone building with a corrugated tin roof is said to date to the 1850s. The same can be said for the other structures in the town. The town was recently purchased by a gentleman, who has been working hard to preserve the history of this tiny village. He was heard saying in an interview on the television show *American Pickers* that he feels the town is still inhabited—he just can't see anyone. There have been documented incidents of paranormal activity in the Cuchillo Bar especially.

Your journey from the interstate will be level for the first leg; you will be surrounded by mountain ranges, which give proof of the volcanic energy that existed in the region millions of years ago. It is this activity that left the deposits of silver, gold, copper, lead, zinc and turquoise for the miners to discover eons later. It was first known as Cuchillo Negro, named after the Apache chief Black Knife, who was killed by the U.S. Cavalry in 1857.

The one-street town contains a church (which will be the first sight you see as you enter town from the east), the Old Cuchillo Bar and approximately twenty occupied residences, along with a few unoccupied original structures,

Cuchillo Bar was once a watering hole for those who were building Elephant Butte Dam.

San Jose church has been rebuilt several times due to flooding.

most of which are located on the right-hand side of the roadway. As there are still residents living in the town, they are concerned with travelers speeding through and have erected signs to warn them. Please obey all speed limits to protect residents, especially the children and pets who may be at risk.

Hillsboro/Kingston

32.92091, -107.56697

Living under the constant threat of the Apache war chief Geronimo, Hillsboro's and Kingston's residents ran a thriving mining district, with rich silver deposits that, in 1882, were worth millions of dollars. This rich ore attracted not only seven thousand miners and prospectors to the town, but it also drew outlaws, ladies of ill repute, gamblers and saloon-owners to loosen the monetary burden of the miners.

Hillsboro was founded in April 1877; it now says it's "a haven for artists, writers and ranchers" and provides a walking tour of its charming downtown area. Starting as a tent city with over three hundred miners, shady ladies, businessmen and children, the town soon began to grow rapidly to include wooden structures. By 1880, the town contained four grocery stores, a post office and, of course, four saloons. Like in its sister city, Kingston, in Hillsboro, the bottom fell out due to the silver panic, but luckily, it had gold mines to rely on as well.

Known as "the gem of the Black Range," Kingston was as wild as anyone could imagine a mining town to be, but it was not without its idiosyncrasies. Miss Sadie Orchard opened her brothel on Virtue Street, most likely as a joke, but she would later take up donations from her clients and those who frequented the saloons for a much-needed church. Sadie also owned the Ocean Grove Hotel in Hillsboro, which is now the Black Range Museum. Memorabilia from Sadie's sordid life and that of her Chinese cook, Tom Ying, with whom she had a tremulous working relationship, are housed in the museum. Pat Garrett, William H. Bonney (also known as Billy the Kid), Lillian Russell and even author Mark Twain were seen in Kingston on occasion.

The Percha Bank Building, now a museum, was one of the busiest spots in town, aside from the saloons. Millions of dollars passed through the building's tall glass and wooden doors. This striking building is the only fully intact building from the wild days of Kingston. Although it stands alone

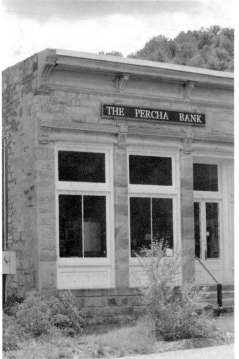

Above: Ruins of the once-impressive Hillsboro Courthouse, which was built in 1898.

Left: Now a museum, the Percha Bank is the only intact building from the mining days in Kingston.

today, Percha Bank Museum was surrounded by other brick structures, as well as the Hillsboro Courthouse and Church. These buildings were destroyed one brick at a time and scattered all around Sierra County by people who took the bricks to use in their own homes and for storefronts in Truth or Consequences.

LAKE VALLEY

36.09168, -108.15729

Gone are the clapboard stores, hotels and saloons of Lake Valley that once stood at attention along the wooden boardwalk where an episode of *Gunsmoke* could easily have been filmed. One of the town's only connections to the outside world came in the form of a stage line driven by Sadie Orchard of Hillsboro fame.

Founded in 1878 as the result of a silver strike founded by a local rancher in 1876, Lake Valley boomed and soon had a population of over four thousand. A school and church were added to the growing number of buildings in the tiny town. These two structures have been restored and

This renovated schoolhouse is now a museum and holds mementos of the past.

The Silver Panic of 1893 destroyed Lake Valley.

preserved by the Bureau of Land Management, which has also stabilized the remaining wooden buildings against collapse.

Lake Valley can be explored in a vehicle or on foot in a self-guided tour. Be sure to visit the school building, which is now a fascinating museum set up in much the same manner as it would have looked in the 1880s. Lining the walls of the museum are vintage photographs of Lake Valley in its prime. Volunteer guides are on premises to relay the history of the town and answer any questions you may have.

The silver deposits that were found in the surrounding Paleozoic limestone were touted to contain some of the purest silver in the United States. The

Crumbling ruins of a town that once held over four thousand people.

Bridal Chamber Mine produced an astounding 2.5 million troy ounces (said to have been indirectly derived from the Roman monetary system), or 78 tons, of silver alone.

To reach the town, travel west from Caballo Lake on NM-153; then turn south onto NM-27. An alternate route would be to travel on NM-26 from the town of Nutt and turn north on NM-27 for approximately twelve miles.

WINSTON

33.34674, -107.64726

After leaving Cuchillo, you will travel along narrow two-lane NM-52, which often will have cows or deer on it as well, so please use caution as you navigate its many dips and turns. The area is also experiencing a lot of flash flooding in the spring and monsoon seasons, so keep an eye out on the weather before and during your travels.

A stop and the Winston General Store at the intersection of NM-52 and Grafton Road is a must. The store carries food items; antiques; collectibles; hunting, RV and camping supplies; books; gifts; laundry and shower supplies; and much more. It is suggested that you fill up on fuel at the store as you explore the mountain roads. The store claims to be the "gateway to the Gila

Winston General Store is a great place to stop on your journey for all your road warrior needs.

Caskets used for the region were made in Frank Winston's Carriage House.

National Forest" and "truly a general store," and it has been touted as "the best remote store in New Mexico."

As you travel slowly through the town of Winston, you will notice some great examples of turn-of-the-century architecture. A square building, on your left-hand side as you travel west on NM-52; has some fine examples of early tinwork, as the corners and curved roof detail are covered in worked squares. This building was originally used as a carriage house for the wealthy Frank Winston when the town was known as Fairview. A small adobe structure behind the carriage house became a casket factory. (An example of one of the caskets made in Winston is kept in the Pioneer Store Museum in Chloride). Diagonally across from the carriage house is Winston's personal residence, which is in the process of being restored.

A kind resident of Winston relayed a story to me about the amount of flooding that still occurs on the Palomas Creek today. He stated a flood once tore through the town in the 1950s, destroying many of the original Fairview structures. A neighbor of his told him she was only four years old at the time and that the fear of a complete devastation of the town was so great, her father tied her and three siblings to a cottonwood tree in the hopes of keeping them from being washed away. One can only imagine the terror that was running through those children's minds as they watched the raging creek rise. Luckily, they all survived to tell the story.

20

HIDALGO COUNTY

SHAKESPEARE

32.32592, -108.73839

Even under the protection of one of the most feared lawmen in the West, the legendary "Dangerous Dan" Tucker, Shakespeare still saw its share of outlaw activity. Vigilante committees were formed and were known to carry out hangings from the sturdy beam in the dining room of the Grant House Saloon, as trees in the area were scarce. So feared was Tucker, it was said Doc Holliday and Wyatt Earp took a different route from Tombstone to the New Mexico Territory in 1882 to avoid any contact with the lawman.

As with most territorial towns, one of Shakespeare's largest threats came from Apache raids, which were often frequent and vicious. The Shakespeare Guard was formed in the late 1880s to protect the town from attack, and it was mostly successful. Gold, copper and silver mining were large sources of income for the town, which boasted three saloons, two blacksmith shops, two hotels, a law office, a mercantile store and a meat market by the early 1880s.

First named Mexican Spring, Shakespeare was also known as Grant and Ralston before 1879, when the Shakespeare Gold Mining and Milling Company took over the failing settlement. Mining was good to the town until the railroad moved through the town of Lordsburg a mere three miles away. Most of the businesses moved that direction as well. The Silver Panic of 1893 shut down the silver mines and put the last nail in Shakespeare's coffin.

One of the oldest photographs of Shakespeare, New Mexico. *Courtesy of the Library of Congress.*

Members of the Wild Bunch, Johnny Ringo and Black Jack Ketchum's gang, would buy supplies in Shakespeare.

In 1907, copper mining in the area brought a few more residents to Shakespeare, but that proved to be short lived as well, and the town fell into disrepair until it was purchased in 1935 by Frank and Rita Hill. The Hills lived on the site and worked day and night to preserve one of the most intact ghost towns in the West. A proud moment occurred in 1970, when the entire town was declared a National Historic Site. Unfortunately, this was also the year Frank Hill passed away, leaving the town to the care of his wife, Rita, and daughter, Janaloo.

Janaloo married Manny Hough in 1984, and Rita passed away in 1985. This passed the torch to the younger generation. The Hough's lived in the General Merchandise Store, which tragically burned down in 1997, along with all of Janaloo's research, photographs and manuscripts. Determined to start again and to keep Shakespeare alive, the couple gave tours of the town dressed in period clothing and sold Janaloo's books to fund their efforts. Janaloo passed away in 2005, and Manny passed in 2018. The town is now in the hands of Manny's daughter Gina and her husband, Dave, who are continuing the noble efforts of Shakespeare's preservation.

STEINS

32.22925, -108.9895

Steins Pass Station near Stein Peak was named after Major Stein, who was rumored to have been killed by Apache in that location (although this was proved false, Steins did participate in a fight against the tribe). The town of Steins (pronounced STEENS), founded in 1880, was then named Doubtful Canyon, as the town was the gateway to one of the most dangerous canyons in New Mexico. (It was "doubtful" you would survive your travels through the canyon.) Since the canyon was a shortcut, many braved the treacherous route, including the Birch Stage Line (lovingly known as Jackass Mail) and the Butterfield Overland Mail. Attacks from the Apache were swift and deadly, so many lost their lives or were captured along the way. Traditionally, the torture of the captives was administered by the Apache women.

Steins became the town's official moniker when the post office was established in 1888. At this time, the town became the official fueling stop for the Southern Pacific Railroad, although the railroad's modern-day location is several miles east of the site of Doubtful Canyon. Gold, silver and copper were discovered in the bootheel of New Mexico, which brought an influx of miners and prospectors to the Arizona border towns. While Steins had only thirty-five registered voters in its books, its population was closer to one hundred. By 1919, with the addition of a dance hall, two bordellos, a boardinghouse, three saloons, a hotel and several stores, the population was closer to one thousand.

When the rock quarry that was used to produce track ballast for the railroad was shut down in 1925, it was the beginning of the end for Steins. It is said Stein had to have water delivered by railroad, since it had no natural resources, so if the deliveries continued, the town could as well. At one dollar per barrel, baths were a luxury.

Shortly after World War II, the Southern Pacific Railroad could not subsidize the delivery of water any longer, so it offered free transportation anywhere to the townspeople. The only catch was that they could only take what they could carry on board, so the homes of the people who took the offer in Stein were left with most of their earthly possessions, turning Stein into a ghost town. Tragically, in 1964, a fire swept through what was left of the town and decimated it, leaving only a few buildings standing. Currently, Stein is owned privately and is being restored, and at one time tours, were offered there. Stein is still evolving. Larry Link, one of the town's last owners, was tragically murdered in front of Steins—this crime is still unsolved.

To access Steins, take the Stein off-ramp from I-10, near the Arizona border. Remains of Steins can be seen north of the interstate when arriving from Arizona.

21

GRANT COUNTY

Piños Altos

32.86341, -108.22144

Outlaw and prospector Robert H. Birch was one of three men who discovered gold in the hills surrounding what became known as Birchville. When Birch, Colonel Snively and a man only known as Hicks stopped to get a drink from the Bear Creek in 1860, they discovered the treasure. Word spread throughout the countryside like wildfire, and soon, there were seven hundred prospectors roaming the Gila Mountains, looking for their share. Conflicts between miners were commonplace as greed set in, but this was also in the middle of the Apache War, which saw the combined forces of War Chiefs Mangas Coloradas and Cochise, approximately three hundred strong, raiding mining camps and killing many.

The Battle of Piños Altos was fought on September 27, 1861, when the Chiricahua army attacked thirty miners who were defending their land. As the Apache's mounted their attack, the captain of the militia forces noticed an old cannon in front of the Sam and Roy (as in Judge Roy Bean) Bean's store. It was moved to a defensive position, filled with nails and buckshot, which was shot at the first wave of attackers. These men were killed instantly, causing the war chiefs to retreat and think the situation over.

Although Piños Altos is shown to have a population of three hundred, most are ranchers in the surrounding mountains. The town once boasted

The Buckhorn Saloon and Opera House is known for its delicious steaks.

Roy Bean operated a mercantile store in Piños Altos before moving to Texas. *Courtesy of the Library of Congress.*

nine thousand residents. The Buckhorn Saloon and Opera House is the main attraction of Piños Altos today; there, you can be served what is touted as one of the finest steak dinners anywhere. The short, seven-mile drive from Silver City is worth the time. You can also visit the Piños Altos Museum and replica of the old fort across the street. For those of you who are rockhounds, this area has outstanding sites to visit.

HANOVER/FIERRO

32.81341, -108.09115

Mainly a Zinc mining town, Hanover was built during World War I to help with the war efforts. Close to the town of Fierro, the two nearly merged during their heydays. A German immigrant came to the area in 1841, discovered zinc, knew its value and began to mine the mineral. Beehive Bar was built 1950 by Emilio Rivera—it was very rough. The bar was located at the top of Snake Hill, west of Hanover (nothing remains). A story called "Devil in the Beehive Bar" circulated; it was about a man who was thrilled to be dancing with a very beautiful woman in the bar, but she turned out to be the devil. Emilio transferred his liquor license to Tyrone and opened the Tyrone Lounge. Hanover is located fifteen minutes away from Silver City. It had a dairy—T.&M. Dairy.

The mines in Fierro (the Spanish word for "iron") pulled 6 million tons of iron out of the surrounding earth while having to endure a run of hard luck, including Apache attacks, deadly mine accidents and fires. Although Fierro boasted a population of over one thousand (mainly individuals of Mexican decent), the Great Depression and World War I took their toll. The mines shut down in 1931 and ran intermittently until the town's focus went toward copper. Before the town's jail was built, if a person became unruly, they would be tied to an eight-foot-tall log until they could behave.

Two main pastimes for the young residents of Fierro were baseball and playing pranks—more specifically tipping outhouses. According to John Mulhouse's *City of Dust* blog, the latter happened on *El dia de las Travesuras*, otherwise known as the Day of Pranks. There is still a good deal of property left to explore in Fierro, although vandals have picked through the town.

GEORGETOWN

32.851186, -108.025318

In 1880, Georgetown's population was just 54, but after silver was discovered in the 1860s, the town grew to a population of approximately 1,200. Named for the vice-president of the Mimbres Mining and Reduction Company George Magruder, Georgetown was able to pull an impressive $3.5 million worth of silver ore from the many mines surrounding the town. Greed would be the downfall to several of Georgetown's residents, who were murdered for their claims and earnings.

Unlike some of the other towns, which were literally thrown together, Georgetown had a plan that included the typical business district, with a bank, hotel, newspaper and several mercantile stores in the center. The next layer included upscale homes, a Catholic church and the schools; the outer layer was where the saloons, houses of ill repute and casinos could be found—literally on the other side of the railroad tracks. The Arizona–New Mexico Railroad placed its tracks through Georgetown in 1891 to make it easier to transport the massive amounts of silver ore to the smelters.

Unfortunately, a chain of disastrous events would lead up to the abandonment of Georgetown by 1903. The first of these events was a fire that swept through the town, followed closely by the smallpox epidemic, which took many of Georgetown's youngest residents. Finally, the Silver Panic of 1893 devastated the entire American Southwest's mining industry, causing Georgetown to be abandoned by 1903.

To reach Georgetown, take NM-152 east from Silver City to the Georgetown Road from Mimbres, New Mexico.

HACHITA/OLD HACHITA

31.91815, -108.32032

Home of several turquoise mine claims, the Old Hachita area is also known for its large rattlesnakes, so please be extremely cautious if you are exploring this region. Established as a mining camp around 1870, the presence of gold, silver, lead, copper and turquoise lured over three hundred people to brave the barren conditions of the southwestern section of New Mexico.

As the mines closed, the El Paso and Southwestern Railway came through a few miles away, sealing the fate of Old Hachita. Oddly enough, the new town was also called Hachita and was built along the railroad tracks.

TYRONE

32.7098, -108.30199

The town of Tyrone was established in 1906 in support of the large discovery of copper and turquoise in the region in 1871. Until 1875, Apache raids forced the town's few miners to leave for safer digs, but the claim was rediscovered by a man known only as Mr. Honeyky who hailed from Tyrone, Ireland—hence the town's new name. By 1909, the Phelps-Dodge Corporation began buying up claims around the towns of Tyrone and its sister city, Leopold, to establish a large copper mining operation.

Sarah Dodge, the wife of one of the Phelps-Dodge Corporation's founders, William E. Dodge Jr., had illusions of grandeur in New Mexico,

Tyrone was financed by the Phelps Dodge Corporation as headquarters for its open-pit copper mine. *Courtesy of the Library of Congress.*

as she set out to make Tyrone on of the most beautiful mining towns in the world. To accomplish her goals, she enlisted the well-known architect Bertram Goodhue, who was famous for designing elaborate exposition and state capitol buildings, to come to the tiny town in southwestern New Mexico to fulfill her dreams.

At the cost of over million in 1915, a Beaux-Arts-inspired business district with a treed plaza, marble drinking fountain, courthouse, hospital, homes, cemetery and a school were built to impress in an ornate Mediterranean style. When the price of copper dropped in 1921, the mines and town closed, and most of the original town site became part of the present-day Tyrone Open-Pit Copper Mine at the cost of $100 million. The mine has been in operation since 1968. Present-day Tyrone is not in the same location as the previous town, and it is the third Tyrone to exist on the site. Large Spanish-style buildings still exist and provide the curious with a great afternoon of exploration of the Beaux-Arts ghost town.

PART V

SOUTHEAST NEW MEXICO

22

LINCOLN COUNTY

Ancho

33.93785, -105.73971

The arrival of the railroad could either enhance or eliminate a western town; in Ancho's case in 1901, the ability to ship tons of product produced by the Ancho Brick Plant was vital to its survival. With the discovery of essential ingredients in brickmaking, namely gypsum and clay, the Ancho plant was in business under the name Gypsum Products Company. The tiny town in southeastern New Mexico came to the rescue of San Francisco during the aftermath of the devastating 1906 earthquake by suppling the ailing city with several tons of bricks to help with the rebuilding efforts.

Only a few remnants of the brick plant and surrounding structures remain today due to the fact when NM-54 was constructed, it bypassed Ancho by a mere two miles. This event caused the Ancho Brick Plant to be closed for good in 1921, which, in turn, started the steady decline of the town. The Ancho School closed in 1955; the train station, which looks to be getting some renovation, followed suit in 1959; and finally, the post office closed in 1969. These derelict buildings were cared for by the diehard residents who remained in the area. The town is now located on private property, but you can still view it and take photographs of Ancho from the fence.

To discover Ancho for yourself, travel south from Socorro, New Mexico, on I-25 to the San Antonio Exit, where you will head east on NM-380 to

Above: The Ancho Brick
Plant sent bricks and
plaster to San Francisco
after the 1906 earthquake
and fire.

Left: Old Ancho School,
as seen from the new
railroad tracks that bisect
the tiny hamlet.

Carrizozo. There, you will turn left onto NM-54 and go 21.9 miles before turning left onto County Road 462. Ancho will be approximately three miles farther down the road.

BONITO CITY

33.45063, -105.70887

This ghost town may have actual ghosts as residents, but they are not there by choice. In 1870, a small group of settlers chose a high mountain meadow as the perfect place to start their town with a group of tents to support the nearby silver mine in the widest part of Bonito Canyon. Since *bonito* means "pretty" in Spanish, it describes the site perfectly. The 1870 gold rush attracted many to the region, as they prospected to make their fortunes.

Supplies were freighted into the mountain community from Las Vegas and White Oaks, New Mexico. Bonito City comprised a saloon run by Peter Nelson, a general store, a school and a post office; it also had a multitude of log homes and cabins, including a boardinghouse operated by William F. and Amanda Yerger Mayberry. The couple had three children, ranging from seven to nineteen years of age in 1874—John William, Edward and Nellie. Most accounts say Nellie was fourteen when the city's tragic incident occurred, but according to genealogical records, she was born in 1874, making her eleven years old.

Bonito City had a stable population—close to five hundred by 1882—and was the scene of a horrific crime that was the opposite of the town's name. Known as the Mayberry Murders by locals, the town was knocked to its knees when the news of the unspeakably senseless crime spread. Although there are several different accounts of how the events of May 5, 1885, occurred, the result was the same, with the deaths of seven townspeople in its aftermath.

A boarder of the Mayberry's, Martin Nelson, a twenty-four-year-old Swedish man who was, for still unknown reasons (but suspected robbery is a likely cause), went berserk, killing his roommate in the boardinghouse, Dr. William H. Flynn of Boston, for his watch fob. It is then thought that Nelson panicked and killed the two young Mayberry boys by shooting them with a .38-caliber rifle and bludgeoning them with the rifle stock to make sure his job was complete. William Mayberry was then shot dead as he rushed to the scene, followed by his wife, Amanda, and daughter, Nellie. Of all

Bonito Lake was drained after it filled with silt and debris from the Little Bear Fire in 2012.

the family members, Nellie was the only one to survive after being shot in the side by Nelson. Amanda Mayberry, in some accounts, was pregnant; although she was mortally shot, she made her way down the front steps of the boardinghouse and to the neighbor's house before being shot once more and passing away.

Pete Nelson (who was not related to the killer) ran from his saloon to intervene and was met with death, as he was also shot and bludgeoned. The local grocer, Herman Beck, peered out of his store at the wrong time and met the same fate. Martin Nelson was said to have escaped into the surrounding mountains after committing this horror, only to return in the morning to see his handiwork. (Other accounts say Beck guarded the Mayberry house after Nelson left town, only to be shot when he returned in the morning.)

It was said in the 1938 account titled "Mayberry Murder Mystery of Bonito City," by A.L. Burke, that Martin Nelson returned to meet his death at the hands of Charlie Berry, who was thought to have been the justice of the peace. According to Burke, the seven victims of this terrible crime were laid out in a row in Pete Nelson's saloon, with the killer's body in the other room.

The Mayberrys, Peter Nelson and Herman Beck were buried on a hillside near Bonito City and later moved to the peaceful little cemetery in Angus forty-five years later to allow for the construction of Bonito Lake, the dam which was built for use by the Southern Pacific Railroad. The common grave for the six victims is marked by a large headstone that was poured on site (the forms were made in El Paso, Texas).

Local legend states that Martin Nelson's body was "deposited" in a hole at the bottom of the hill where the original graves were located; he was buried face-down, pointing west "to ensure his spirit would not rise and walk the Earth." Nelson was reinterred about fifty feet above the road on a hillside east of the Angus Cemetery; it is overgrown and forgotten today, even though there is a concrete headstone.

Due to the gruesome nature of these crimes, the log boardinghouse stood empty for fifteen years before it was torn down forty-five years later, along with the rest of the town. The structure became the source of local ghost stories, strange happenings and paranormal sightings. Strange accounts have been reported even today, after the demolition of the remnants of the town.

Today, the meager foundations of the town lie below Bonito Lake, which served as

Victims of the Bonito City Massacre were buried in a mass grave in Angus Cemetery.

the primary potable water source for the community of Alamogordo forty miles down the mountain. They were uncovered when massive cleanup efforts were required after the Little Bear Forest Fire of 2012, which left Bonito Lake saturated with over twelve feet of soot, debris and burned logs. Another water source had to be found for Alamogordo.

Jicarilla

33.86896, -105.66304

Travel twelve miles northeast of the ghost town of White Oaks, and you will find the remains of the settlement of Jicarilla (Hic-Caw-REE-ah), which, amazingly, had a lifespan of fifty years, from 1892 to 1942, after the discovery of gold and coal in the Jicarilla Mountains. The wooden post office with a tin roof, established in 1892 and serving until 1927, is still standing, as is the log schoolhouse and remnants of a brick store. They are all under the management of the Bureau of Land Management. Mexican batea bowls were used to pan the gold-laden dirt, as several hundred prospectors came to the town. The population rose dramatically during the Great Depression, since the mining operations were paying higher wages than larger towns. But once the gold played out, residents moved on to better prospects. Mining is still being done in the Jicarilla Mountains today.

White Oaks

33.7476, -105.7364

As you drive along the narrow two-lane roadway heading to White Oaks, it is easy to imagine the settlement being a bustling community at one time. Cattle lazily graze on the gramma grass in the plains along your route. As you turn the corner and slowly ascend into the foothills of Lincoln National Forest, remnants of tailing piles are visible on the slopes of Baxter Mountain.

One of the biggest surprises may be the Victorian architecture of the remaining buildings that made up the town, which is far from the traditional New Mexican adobe style found everywhere. One of the most impressive of the homes is the Hoyle Mansion, which was built in 1893 by Matthew "Watt" Hoyle, one of the owners of the Old Abe Mine. This beautiful brick

Left: The tragic Hoyle Mansion graces the landscape with its Victorian beauty.

Below: As a mining town, a saloon or three were essential. The No Scum Allowed Saloon is still a booming business.

home with a metal widow's walk was to be the home of Hoyle and his future bride (rumored to be a mail-order bride), and no expense was spared. It was said to have cost between $40,000 and $70,000, using imported Italian marble, mahogany wall paneling and mantles, leaded glass windows and every amenity available at that time.

Two stories make up the next part of Watt's saga. The first states that Hoyle's fiancée made the journey to New Mexico from the East Coast, making it as far as St. Louis, Missouri, before deciding she was not going to continue any farther. The next part says the lady arrived in White Oaks, saw how rugged the lifestyle was and promptly left Watt and the state forever.

Following these events, the stately home became known as "Hoyle's Folly," and the interior was said to have never been completed. But an article describing a housewarming party thrown in Hoyle's honor in October 1893 states differently. Urban legends say Hoyle was so heartbroken that he left the home, never to be seen again. Others say he threw himself into the north side of the Old Abe Mine. But Hoyle lived in the house with his older brother Will and Will's wife. After the gold played out, the Exchange Bank of Carrizozo, New Mexico, seized the property in June 1908 to cover delinquent taxes. Hoyle had moved to Denver by this time. Either way, it is a truly sad tale for such an impressive home. Records show Matthew Hoyle married Sarah Belle Dengey in Boulder, Colorado, in April 1916 at the age of fifty (his bride was forty-six). Matthew Hoyle would pass away on October 3, 1941, at the age of ninety-five.

William H. Bonney, the infamous Billy the Kid, was known to frequent White Oak's many saloons and play cards with his friend Pat Garrett. As a highly recognized leader of a cattle-rustling group in the hills surrounding White Oaks, Billy was often run out of town by the local authorities. The No Scum Allowed Saloon still operates in the town and does booming business on the weekends, as it's popular with the weekend travelers and motorcyclists alike. Music from the patio fills the valley with life.

23

CHAVES COUNTY

Acme/Frazier

33.59232, -104.32858

As you take NM-70 east, you will pass a beautiful rock structure on the left-hand side of the road on the way to Portales. This was the schoolhouse for the town of Frazier. The community of Acme had a post office from 1906 to 1946. Located on the side of the highway, seventeen miles from the city of Roswell, near the Salt Creek Wilderness area, the schoolhouse breaks up the stark landscape surrounding it.

The rock construction of Frazier is well done, with a pair of rock arches leading to the equally impressive stone building. Weeds and broken glass—and maybe a couple of lizards—are all that occupy the school today. Children were charged with providing their own books, supplies and lunches for school, which taught first through eighth graders. In 1907, before the rock school was built, classes were held in a tent in Acme.

Acme boasted a hotel, train depot, a general store and a large horse barn, all built to service the Acme Gypsum Cement Company. Acme had a population of forty, with twenty of them being children (making the Frazier school necessary). The school building also served as a church and was the site of funeral services. It was the last one-teacher school built in Chaves County. The number of students attending Frazier school dropped below the mandatory eight, so the remaining children had to attend school in Roswell.

The Frazier Rock Schoolhouse has stood the tests of time in the desert.

Relics of the Acme Gypsum Cement Company are slowing eroding away.

A small cemetery lies approximately fifty yards to the west of the school building and appears to be largely unattended, lonely and overgrown. It contains several families of former Frazier/Acme residents. One of the most heartbreaking rows includes a row of tiny headstones belonging to infants and their parents who passed within a short time of each other.

After the cement factory closed, ranching became a large industry, it included cattle, sheep, and turkey. Rabbit and coyotes were herded for their pelts just so the ranchers could survive.

Blackdom

33.1637167, -104.5088556

This community established twenty miles south of Roswell, New Mexico, had the distinction of being New Mexico's first Black settlement. Blackdom's founder, Francis Marion Boyer, was said to have been escaping threats from the Ku Klux Klan in Georgia whenever he established an all-Black community comprising thirteen families in the early 1900s. While attending Morehouse College and Fish University, Boyer learned about homesteading requirements. He received his homesteading patent in 1908. Also, by 1908, the town had a population of over three hundred and supported a newspaper, church and other businesses necessary for its existence. With a combined investment of $10,000, the families were able to settle and own 13,056 acres in the New Mexico desert.

Primarily a farming community, Blackdom was dependent on the availability of water. Southeastern New Mexico is notorious for its droughts and lack of surface water, so the population dwindled substantially by the start of the Great Depression in the late 1920s, mainly due to crop failure.

According to an article written for *Smithsonian Magazine* by Leah Binkovitz, in a December 1912 letter to the editor of the Black newspaper, the *Chicago Defender*, Blackdom resident Lucy Henderson wrote: "Here, the Black man has an equal chance with the White man. Here, you are reckoned at the value which you place upon yourself. Your future is in your hands." When asked why she wrote the letter, she stated, "I feel I owe it to my people to tell them of this free land out here." Henderson also relayed the fact that Blackdom sported a post office, store, school, pumping plant and residences, as well as the church and newspaper. She was so enthusiastic in her promotion of Blackdom, Henderson assured anyone willing to take a chance by moving to New Mexico that they would "never have cause to regret it."

Boyer's journey to New Mexico from Georgia was a dangerous one and was done all on foot. He had heard about New Mexico from his father, a buffalo soldier who had visited the land during the Mexican American War. It is reported that the Pacific Mutual Company believed in Boyer's dream enough to loan him money to dig a well so he could begin farming. Surviving pieces of Blackdom's stationary reads, "Blackdom Townsite Co., Roswell, New Mexico. The only exclusive Negro settlement in New Mexico." This was a proud moment for Boyer and the families who settled in the area.

Since Frank and his wife, Ella Boyer, were both college-educated, they made sure education was a priority in Blackdom and were quick to establish a school, which was first housed in the church. The Boyers knew the importance of teaching their students Black history as a pathway to empower future generations. The Boyer family would eventually move on to establish their second town named Vado in the Mesilla Valley of Doña Ana County, south of Las Cruces on the east side of the Rio Grande in 1921. This town also served as the place of Frank's death. Frank Boyer was buried in Vado Riverview Cemetery in Vado. Another investor of Blackdom fame was Mattie (or Mittie) Moore Wilson, an infamous madame who established an empire in Chaves County

All that remains of this unique town are a few foundations and a historical marker touting the history of Blackdom. The town closed its post office in 1919. Although farming did not work out for the settlement, in 1920, large deposits of oil were discovered in the Roswell region. Blackdom residents pooled their resources together to form the Blackdom Oil Company, which controlled about ten thousand acres. In March 1920, the company entered a contract for 4,200 acres with the National Exploration Company in a deal worth upward of $70,000. Unfortunately, the oil fields were not commercially viable, and oil activity dried up to move farther south from the Roswell Basin to the Permian Basin near Carlsbad, New Mexico. This move was the final act for Blackdom, which did not survive the Great Depression.

Boaz

33.73676, -103.97135

Started—like many communities in New Mexico—as a blind-siding railroad support town, Boaz is located thirty-seven miles northeast of Roswell and forty-nine miles southwest of Portales. When the Pecos Valley and Northeast Railroad (which was lovingly referred to as the "Pea Vine" in the region) was built in 1899 by James J. Hagerman and associates at a cost of $750,000 to form a line from Amarillo, Texas, to Roswell, New Mexico, the town of Boaz sprang forth around 1903. Products shipped by rail from Boaz included bear grass (ten boxcars a year of baled bear grass, which grew in great abundance around the town, were shipped), rabbits (by the thousands, shipped to Amarillo) and eggs, milk and cream.

Advertisements sent east, touted huge homesteads available in the Boaz area, so a passenger service was added to the Pea Vine and was dubbed the "Doodle Bug" Train. Potential homesteaders arrived in Boaz with all their worldly possessions, including livestock, to offload them onto wagons so everything could be taken to their new homes. This service was phased out in the 1950s, when the railroad gave way to other means of transportation, such as automobiles and aircraft.

By 1910, there were 150 souls living in Boaz and the surrounding area. The town boasted a school, which possibly doubled as a church, a two-story store with apartment and cellar, a blacksmith shop, a bank, a lumber yard, three livery stables, stockyards, numerous homestead shacks, a post office, a hotel and, of course, a clapboard railway depot. The name Boaz was thought to have been a biblical reference, as Boaz was the second husband of Ruth and names from the Bible were commonly used to name towns. Boaz was also described as a wealthy and benevolent man, and it was the hope of the townspeople that their location would reflect this description.

Boaz was originally platted with four streets running north–south and four east–west; these were each sixty feet wide. As the town expanded, another four streets, or forty acres, were added. These additions were separated from each other as they were bisected by the railway. Although the town was a support for the railroad, most of the residents described themselves as farmers or ranchers.

A cemetery lies approximately three-quarters of a mile west of the Boaz townsite and includes at least twenty-four graves dating from 1910, but only eight are identifiable, with the last grave being placed in 1952.

Delphos

34.075361, -103.492457

Built in 1903 as a watering station for the Santa Fe Railroad Company, Delphos was not considered a formal railroad station. A large barn was utilized at Delphos to store items for shipping to Roswell and Portales. The townsite of forty acres, with sixteen blocks, comprised a store, a post office, several homes and a service station, which was running until the 1950s. There is also evidence along U.S.-70 of a small café in operation in the 1970s, but the town had played out by 1975. Many of the structures were moved to nearby Kenna or nearby ranches. According to Harding Polk II, David A. Phillips Jr. and Marie E. Brown in their "Archaeological and Historical Studies Along U.S. 70 Between Roswell and Portales, New Mexico" report, Delphos "represents a failed dream." Unfortunately, this could be said for most of the small railroad towns that were formed along the rails with big hopes.

24

LEA COUNTY

Antioch

33.0673, -103.1005

Sixteen miles northwest of Lovington and three miles west of the Texas state line is a small cemetery that was used for the town of Antioch (originally known as Midway). An old church on Fillingim Road is all that remains of the little town on the plains of southeastern New Mexico, which included a store, a post office and a school at one time. Look for the cemetery marker sign on the highway. The young daughter of homesteaders Wiley and Lula Doran was the first to be buried on the church grounds in 1910. Many of those buried the small graveyard were homesteaders, as well as veterans of the Civil and Spanish-American Wars, World Wars I and II and the Korean and Vietnam Wars.

Knowles

32.84039, -103.12771

Twenty-eight miles outside of Hobbs, New Mexico, sits the town of Knowles, which was established in 1903 by Rube or Ben L. (depending on source) Knowles, who came from Monument. Lea County's historian stated

Knowles was Lea County's second city to be founded after Monument and was at one time the largest, with a population of five hundred at its peak. A post office and store were opened in the small town, but soon, a saloon, blacksmith shop, bank, two-story hotel and newspaper office followed.

Due to a survey error, Knowles was once part of Eddy County, but when the adjustment was made, the town returned to Lea County. Sporting a two-story hotel, which was known to have both horses and buggies and Ford Model T passenger cars parked in front, Knowles had a population of five hundred and had the largest population in Lea County in its early days.

The Knowles Cemetery, which is also known as the Old Teague Cemetery, is surrounded by farmland and is the only remnant of the once-bustling town that raised a ruckus north of Hobbs on Knowles Road.

MALJAMAR

32.85643, -103.76322

Formed from the combination of the names Malcolm, Janet and Margaret (the children of the town's founder, William Mitchell), Maljamar was the site of the first oilwell in southeastern New Mexico. The well was brought in by the Maljamar Oil and Gas Company, of which William Mitchell was the president in 1926. Located approximately twenty-six miles west of Lovington, New Mexico, Maljamar was founded in 1943 and soon saw a Baptist church, oil field service companies, a café and a service station be built to support the town.

The plains of southeastern New Mexico, also known as the Llano Estacado, were home to many tribes of Natives, who roamed the area. Pottery shards of Chupadero Black-and-White, Three Rivers Red Wash, El Paso Polychrome and La Junta Focus earthenware dating to around 1300 CE have been found by archaeologists in the sand dunes surrounding the town of Maljamar. These are evidence of the diverse groups of people who called the plains home.

OIL CENTER

32.49929, -103.26131

Also known by the name Crile-McIntyre, the town of Oil Center is located between Monument and Eunice, New Mexico. Built in the early 1930s, Oil Center was promoted by the Singleton-Crile Township Company and was first named McIntyre. It had an active post office until December 1994, although the town saw its demise in 1986. While driving north–south on NM-8, you will notice a gas station on the right, a grocery store and post office on the left, as well as a few homes—all in a rough state of disrepair.

Oil Center was developed to support the booming oil and gas industry in Lea County, as large amounts of oil companies flooded the area with their workers. It was later named Oil Center due to the large Phillips Petroleum and El Paso Natural Gas Plants housed there. Today, ironically, the only building representing Oil Center is an old gas station.

25

EDDY COUNTY

CUBA

32.3512, -104.1686 (Otis)

In a flat, windswept scrub brush–filled field on West London Road, near Otis, New Mexico, sits the only reminder of the town of Cuba in the southeastern part of the state: its cemetery. (Note: there is also a Cuba, New Mexico, in Sandoval County on NM-550, north of Albuquerque.) If not for the metal sign that designates this lonely stretch of land as an Official Eddy County Historical Site, most would not know of its existence.

The United States government was giving land grants to anyone who was willing to settle in this desolate region in 1910; as a result, many Hispanic families from Shafter, Texas (located south of Marfa, Texas), took advantage of the opportunity. Farming in the dry, rocky soil for a meager existence was hard enough, but when the influenza outbreak of 1918 occurred, the entire town was nearly wiped out. There are an estimated five hundred

The Spanish influenza epidemic of 1918 wiped out the entire town of Cuba.

CUBA CEMETERY PLOT

Few records exist concerning Cuba, the small Hispanic community that sat near this cemetery plot from 1890 to about 1930. Tradition says that several of the original settlers came to this place following closure of the silver mines at Shafter, Texas, about 1890. A later wave of families arrived during the Mexican Revolution of 1917. Most of these families found work on the valley farms, and several successfully homesteaded their own allotments of government patent land in the surrounding area.

The community, for a period of time, had its own general store and one-room school. People from across the valley periodically came to witness its famous horse races. It is said that the deadly worldwide influenza epidemic of 1918 virtually wiped out the community. In the decade following that tragedy its remaining members began to move elsewhere.

This 3.2 acre cemetery plot was donated to the community for that purpose by one of the settlers. The cemetery continued to be used for occasional burials until the 1940's. In June, 1994, this land was transferred to the County of Eddy, and the Mexican Cemetery Association today oversees the cemetery and advises the Eddy County Commission on any facility needs.

It is estimated there are over five hundred graves in the cemetery, but the locations of only thirty-eight are known.

graves in the Cuba Cemetery, but unfortunately, only about forty of those are identifiable.

When the land and cemetery fell to ruins, the Mexican Cemetery Association took an interest in them and petitioned the Eddy County Commissioners to take control of the site. The county agreed by installing a fence, watering system and monument at the cemetery. As of today, the Mexico Cemetery Association is still working diligently to identify the people who call this plot of land their final resting place.

Dayton

32.74315, -104.38524

This community was founded in 1902 by J.C. Day as a farming community northwest of the Rio Peñasco. The entire town of Dayton, with the exception of the post office and a store, was moved a short time later, in the winter of 1904, to a location eight miles south of Artesia, New Mexico and one mile west of the railroad tracks. Dayton grew to include a prosperous bank, two churches, a hotel, school, newspaper and other businesses, including an automatic service garage. Today, all that remains of the town is the wooden shell of the service station, which is leaning precariously on an old tree stump. Other buildings that belonged to Dayton have recently been torn down, with the land being relinquished to the alfalfa crops.

Due to the existence of Artesian springs and an irrigation system developed by Pat Garrett (famous for gunning down Billy the Kid) in the area, Dayton was known to produce "splendid crops" of alfalfa. In 1909, it was reported that forty acres of alfalfa produced $1,000 worth of crops. Irrigation systems were a huge factor in the growth of not only the crops but also the town. In nearby Lakewood, a tomato canning factory became a major employer of the women of Eddy County, including those in Dayton.

The discovery of oil near Dayton in 1913 was the first of its kind in Eddy County. Dubbed the Brown Oil Well, it produced fifty-two gallons, or approximately one barrel, of oil per day. A town named Oil City, located a few miles southwest of Dayton, sprang up to support the new oil industry in 1914. A large "gusher" strike occurred near Artesia in 1919, when Martin Yates Jr.'s oil well known as Illinois No. 3 spewed forth the black gold to start an extremely lucrative oil industry in southeastern New Mexico.

The last structure of Dayton leans precariously on an old stump for support.

Dayton's newspaper, the *Pecos Valley Echo*, was said to have been one of the most enterprising newspapers in the Pecos Valley. It was reported that by 1925, most of the houses from Dayton and Lakewood had been moved to Carlsbad, New Mexico, twenty-four miles away. During this time, Carlsbad was experiencing a boom, due to the discovery of potash east of town, and it was hoped these houses, once they were renovated, would relieve the need for rentals. By 1912, the *Pecos Valley Echo* was renamed the *Dayton Informer*. In 1916, the beautiful Dayton Depot burned to the ground due to unknown causes, and with it, the hopes of Dayton diminished as well. Unfortunately, several of the remaining structures of Dayton have been razed, nearly causing the town to vanish completely.

LOOKOUT

32.2315, -104.1094

As a viable community, Lookout was on a mail stage route from Pecos, Texas, to Roswell, New Mexico, until the mid-1900s. Since there was an easy crossing of the Pecos and Black Rivers nearby, Lookout also saw many cattle run along the trails that stretched from Texas to Kansas. Jesse J. Rascoe was the first to see a need for a settlement on the spot near modern-day Malaga, New Mexico. Since wood was scarce and had to be freighted eighty-eight miles from Toyah, Texas, the residents of Lookout lived in dugouts that they hollowed out along the banks of Black River.

As with many towns in early New Mexico, the railroad dictated Lookout's survival. In Lookout's case, its population boomed to 350 by late 1885, but this prosperity would not continue, as the railroad bypassed the tiny community to run a line through the villages of Loving and Malaga. Many of Lookout's citizens then relocated to one of these neighboring towns. Between the railroad and the typhoid breakout of 1909, Lookout was reduced to a ghost town early on. All that remains of Lookout is a dilapidated cemetery, with old wooden crosses bearing the names of the deceased unable to be read. Even the concrete markers are unreadable, and others have only a date or initials. The graves date from as early as 1899 to as recently as 1995, as it contains many family plots.

The cemetery is on private land but can be accessed through a gate. Take NM-285 to Pecos from Loving's city limits for three-tenths of a mile and turn right onto CR-716 (also known as Higby Hole Road). Travel 2.2 miles south, turn right onto CR-718 (also known as Ogden Road). From there, travel another three-tenths of a mile to a dirt road on the left with a gate—this is the private property, but the gate is left unlocked. Be sure to close the gate after you enter and exit. Follow the private farm road to two other gates that are side by side. Enter the gate on the left and continue south; there, you will see the cemetery on the left side of the road, approximately six-tenths of a mile from Ogden Road.

QUEEN

32.19094, -104.74579

The Lincoln National Forest is ruggedly beautiful, with limestone outcroppings and cliffs and piñon, juniper and ponderosa pines scattered throughout the landscape providing great venues for hunting, hiking and camping. The forest is also home to Queen, New Mexico, which is widely lauded as being the home of southern New Mexico's best green chile cheeseburger. Forty-five minutes from the city of Carlsbad, Queen has few residents to compete with the deer and cattle, but it has a rich history.

A memorial to the "Paperboy of the Guadalupes" after his plane crashed in Queen, New Mexico.

Elias G. Queen donated part of his ranch, which he and his family had established in 1898, for J.W. Tulk to build a store and post office. This plot also included the only water in the area. With this donation, the town was then known as Queen in 1905. As a ranching community, the town relied heavily on rainfall and grass abundance for success. In 1920, the ranching in the rocky mountain area declined, leaving the town to fall to ruin. Today, only a rock chimney remains of any of the original buildings.

In the spring of 1964, a few miles from the café in Queen, one of the most well-loved characters of the region flew Reverend Willis E. Plapp in to give sunrise services for the members of the Pecos Valley Trail Ride. Frank Kindel was known as "Mr. Carlsbad," since he was always promoting the town he loved. You could see Mr. Kindel riding a unicycle in the local parades or doing what he was also famous for: being the "Paperboy of the Guadalupe's," as he utilized his Piper airplane to deliver mail and newspapers to the isolated ranchers in the Guadalupe Mountains. (There are no reports on how the items fared when they hit the ground.)

After the service, Reverend Plapp and Mr. Kindel only made it a few miles before Kindel's plane crashed for unknown reasons. Reverend Plapp experienced serious injuries and recovered, but tragically, Frank Kindel perished with his plane. A memorial monument for the Paper Boy of the Guadalupe's now stands only feet from the crash site. Mr. Kindel was mourned by the entire town of Carlsbad.

26

OTERO COUNTY

BRICE

32.37111, -106.08389 (Oro Grande)

About a quarter of a mile north of Oro Grande, along an old railway, is the mining town of Brice. Not much is left of this once-bustling community, but there are a few buildings, several mine shafts and a barely discernable graveyard with one wooden cross and an upright headstone. First called Jarilla, after the nearby Jarilla Mountains, Brice was witness to the discovery of an amazing six-ounce gold nugget at the Nannie Baird Mine in 1898.

Turquoise was also a big producer, along with copper and iron, and had been mined by the local tribes for several hundred years before the westerners moved in. Amos J. Meules is credited with "rediscovering" the turquoise deposits in the early 1890s. Brice was the first encampment to work the copper, lead, silver and gold deposits in the district.

By 1904, Brice sported a general store, schoolhouse, a hotel, a post office, a saloon and four mining companies, with a population of 150 that had doubled by 1919. When a railroad spur was run to the nearby town of Alvin, a smelter was built in Oro Grande to process the gold, copper and iron ores being pulled from the local mines.

Brice is located approximately one-quarter of mile north of Oro Grande on U.S.-54. Turn left after the Oro Grande limit sign and go approximately three miles on the old railroad bed. Buildings are visible from NM-54, near the new mining operations.

ORO GRANDE

32.37111, -106.08389

Nestled thirty-six miles south of Alamogordo on U.S.-54, Oro Grande consists mainly of an old schoolhouse today. It sits about one hundred yards off the highway. Once known as Jarilla Junction when it was used as a station for the El Paso and Northeastern Railroad, the small mining town gained its moniker "Big Gold" when a gold nugget that was reportedly the size of a man's finger was discovered in 1905. Although the Jarilla Mountains had been used for prospecting since 1879, this enormous find set off a gold rush in the area. J.M. Perkins is given credit for being the first prospector in the Oro Grande region in 1879, but Oro Grande never lived up to its name. Perkin's was said to have given up his claim for two barrels of water for unknown reasons.

In 1898, Oliver Lee, one of the more notable characters of the region, was tried in Hillsboro for the murder and disappearance of Colonel Albert

Gold mining in Oro Grande (meaning "Big Gold") did not live up to the name. *Courtesy of the Library of Congress.*

Jennings Fountain and his eight-year-old son, Henry. Lee was a well-known opponent of the outlaw Billy the Kid, who Fountain had as a client. Lee was acquitted of the crime.

The population of Oro Grande swelled to the thousands, as people set out to find their fortunes in Otero County. This made the tiny town the center of the mining industry. A fifty-five-mile-long water pipe constructed from the Sacramento River to Oro Grande and set up by the Southwestern Smelting and Refining Company in 1907 allowed an immediate growth, and the construction of homes began with a vengeance. The carpenters could not keep up with the astounding growth, which meant many had to live in canvas tents and shanties.

A smelter was added to the town in November 1907, which drew more prospectors and miners to the Oro Grande area. But as it did in many other towns, the grade and quantity of ore began to faulter, leading to the smelter being shut down six months later. Having been sold soon after shutting down, it was reopened in 1910. It is estimated that $2 million worth of ore was recovered from Oro Grande Mining District.

In addition to gold, prospectors were finding deposits of copper, iron, silver and turquoise, which sustained the town for a few years until it began to wane, causing the investors and promoters to pull out of the area. The town then reverted to a railroad community.

Mining continues today in the Jarilla Mountains as new claims become available. The mining district roads and terrain are rough, so it is good to use caution when visiting. Surrounded by the White Sands Missile Range to the west and the McGregor Artillery Range on its southern and eastern sides, Oro Grande is a little over fifty miles from the center of El Paso, Texas, and Fort Bliss. As you arrive from Alamogordo, New Mexico, you will notice the older section of town on the right and the newer section on the left. There is a gas station and convenience store available.

27

ROOSEVELT COUNTY

CAUSEY

33.8793, -103.1266

Perched at the crossroads of NM-114 and NM-321, approximately thirty-five miles southeast of Portales, New Mexico, and only one mile from the Texas border, Causey has a long history. The open plains of grasslands that surround Causey, otherwise known as the Llano Estacado, were havens for huge herds of bison that roamed Texas and New Mexico.

According to author John Mulhouse, it is thought the town received its name from two brothers, T.L. "George" and John Causey, who lived in the area and were renowned buffalo hunters—especially George. George's hunting buddy George Jefferson is quoted as saying, "Causey killed more buffalo in one winter than Buffalo Bill Cody killed in his entire lifetime." The number was said to be a stunning forty thousand animals. Causey was said to have shot the last buffalo on the Llano Estacado in 1882.

KENNA

33.8423, -103.7719

Beginning as a cattle shipping point, Kenna was established after the Civil War in 1884, along the Atchison, Topeka and Santa Fe Railway. Stockyards

Close to the Texas border, Kenna was a cattle shipping hub.

lined the tracks, giving the air what some New Mexicans call "the sweet smell of success"—others may not be so generous with the term. The town was originally known as Urton, after the Missouri contractor brothers who were first in the area. Another contractor named E.D. Kenna, the vice-president of the railroad, set up camp in Urton during the construction of the railroad, and this camp became a stage stop with a postal exchange. At the completion of the railway in 1899, Kenna became the official name of the camp. The name reverted to Urton in 1902, with the opening of the post office, but by 1906, the townsite was once again referred to as the Kenna Development Company.

One hundred miles from Roswell, New Mexico, on NM-70, Kenna is one of many ghost towns that litter this stretch of roadway. On your way, you will encounter Acme/Frazier, Elkins and Boaz, which are mentioned in this book. Nestled in a valley, Kenna is considered not exactly impressive, but in its youth, Kenna was home to over two thousand residents, two hotels, a bank, several stores, a post office and, naturally, with so many cowboys to man the stockyards, several saloons.

BIBLIOGRAPHY

Baxter, William. *Gold and the Ortiz Mine Grant: A New Mexico History and Reference Guide*. Santa Fe, NM: Lone Butte Press, 2014.

Beck, Warren A., and Ynez D. Haase. *Historical Atlas of New Mexico*. Norman: University of Oklahoma Press, 1989.

Burke, A.L., and Floy W. Skinner. *The Mayberry Murder Mystery of Bonito City*. Nogal, NM: Alamogordo Press, 1938.

Burney, Michael S. *Historical Archaeology of the Big Five Gold Mine: Excavations Along Bitter Creek, Northeast of the Town of Red River, Taos County, New Mexico*. Sunnyvale, CA: LAP Lambert Academic Publishing, 2014.

Carpenter, Cindy, and Sherry Fletcher. *Images of America: Hatch Valley*. Charleston, SC: Arcadia Publishing, 2015.

Church, Peggy Pond. *The House at Otowi Bridge: The Story of Edith Warner and Los Alamos*. Albuquerque, NM: University of New Mexico Press, 1973.

Cozzens, Gary. *The Nogal Mesa: A History of Kivas and Ranchers in Lincoln County*. Charleston, SC: The History Press, 2011.

Editors of *Sunset Magazine*. *Ghost Towns of the West*. Menlo Park, CA: Lane Publishing Co., 1978.

Flores, Daniel B. *Cuento de La Pintada: Stories of a Guadalupe County Village*. Scotts Valley, CA: CreateSpace, 2014.

Frantz, Laurie Evans. *The Turquoise Trail*. Images of America. Charleston, SC: Arcadia Publishing, 2013.

Harris, Linda. *Ghost Towns Alive: Trips to New Mexico's Past*. Albuquerque: University of New Mexico Press, 2003.

Hillsboro Historical Society. *Around Hillsboro*. Images of America. Charleston, SC: Arcadia Publishing, 2011.

———. *Sadie Orchard: Madam of New Mexico's Black Range*. Hillsboro, NM: Hillsboro Historical Society, 2019.

Jones, Robert C. *Ghost Towns, Forts and Pueblos of New Mexico*. Kennesaw, GA: Self-published, 2004.

Julyan, Robert. *The Place Names of New Mexico*. Albuquerque: University of New Mexico Press, 1998.

Keleher, William A. *The Fabulous Frontier: Twelve New Mexico Items*. Santa Fe, NM: Rydal Press, 1942.

Kutz, Jack. *Mysteries and Miracles of New Mexico*. Randolph, MA: Rhombus Publishing, 1988.

Looney, Ralph. *Haunted Highways: The Ghost Towns of New Mexico*. Albuquerque: University of New Mexico Press, 1979.

Lyon-Cline, Jody. *Ghosts of Piños Altos*. Piños Altos, NM: Self-published, 2001.

McDuff, Leon. *Tererro*. Bloomington, IN: Trafford Publishing, 2007.

McLemore, Virginia T. *Silver and Gold in New Mexico*. Socorro: New Mexico Bureau of Geology and Mineral Resources, 2001.

Miller, Rod. *The Lost Frontier: Momentous Moments in the Old West You May Have Missed*. Guilford, CT: TwoDot, 2015.

Mulhouse, John M. *America Through Time: Abandoned New Mexico: Ghost Towns, Endangered Architecture, and Hidden History*. Charleston, SC: America Through Time, 2020.

Parker, Morris B. *White Oaks: Life in a New Mexico Gold Camp, 1880–1900*. Tucson: University of Arizona Press, 1971.

Pearce, T.M. *New Mexico Place Names: A Geographical Dictionary*. Albuquerque: University of New Mexico Press, 1965.

Polk, Harding, II, David A. Phillips and Marie E. Brown. *Archaeological and Historical Studies Along U.S. 70 Between Roswell and Portales, New Mexico*. Historic Homesteads and Towns. Volume 2. NMDOT Cultural Resource Technical Series no. 2003-2: SWCA project no. 3835-0008, SWCA report no. 02-265. Santa Fe, NM: State of New Mexico, 2004.

Rakocy, Bill. *Ghosts of Kingston, Hillsboro, New Mexico*. El Paso, TX: Bravo Press, 1983.

Sherman, James E. *Ghost Towns and Mining Camps of New Mexico*. Norman: University of Oklahoma Press, 1975.

Simmons, Marc. *Treasure Trails of the Southwest*. Albuquerque: University of New Mexico Press, 1994.

Siringo, Charlie. *A Cowboy Detective: A True Story of Twenty-Two Years with a World-Famous Detective Agency*. Lincoln, NE: Bison Books, 1988.

Stanley, F. *A White Oaks Story*. Pep, TX: Self-published, 1966.

Varney, Philip. *New Mexico's Best Ghost Towns: A Practical Guide*. Albuquerque: University of New Mexico Press, 1981.

Woods, Betty. *The Press of the Territorian Presents Number 4 of a Series of Western Americana: Ghost Towns and How to Get to Them*. Santa Fe, NM: Press of the Territorian, 1969.

WPA. *New Mexico: A Guide to the Colorful State: Complied by Workers of the Writer's Program of the Work Projects Administration of the State of New Mexico*. New York: Hastings House, 1940.

ARTICLES

Binkovitz, Leah. "Welcome to Blackdom: The Ghost Town That Was New Mexico's First Black Settlement; A Homesteading Settlement Founded Out of Reach of Jim Crow Is Now a Ghost Town, but Postal Records Live On to Tell Its Story." *Smithsonian Magazine*, February 4, 2013. www.smithsonianmagazine.com.

INDEX

W

Wagon Mound, New Mexico 23, 53
Watrous, New Mexico 70, 72
Watrous, Samuel B. 72
White Oaks, New Mexico 41, 50,
        152, 154
Whittington Center 63
Winston, Frank 134
Winston General Store 133
Winston, New Mexico 133, 134

Y

Yeso, New Mexico 89, 90

ABOUT THE AUTHOR

Exploring her home state of New Mexico is author Donna Blake Birchell's favorite pastime. Sharing what she has found gives her great joy, and she hopes you will find as much enjoyment in your own treks of discovery in the Land of Enchantment.